Overcoming
Guide

Other books by Elizabeth McMahon

Virtual Reality Therapy for Anxiety: Therapist Guide
with Debra Boeldt, PhD (in press)

Overcoming the Emotional Challenges of Lymphedema

Lymphedema and Lipedema Nutrition Guide
with Chuck Ehrlich, Emily Iker, MD, Karen Herbst, PhD, MD, Linda-Anne
Kahn, CLT-LANA, Dorothy D. Sears, PhD, Mandy Kenyon, MS, RD, CSSD

Lymphedema Caregiver's Guide
with Mary Kathleen Kearse, PT, CLT-LANA, and Ann Ehrlich, MA

Voices of Lymphedema
editor with Ann B. Ehrlich

Living Well With Lymphedema
with Ann Ehrlich and Alma Vinjé-Harrewijn, PT, CLT-LANA

Overcoming
Anxiety and Panic
interactive guide

Elizabeth McMahon, PhD

Hands-on-Guide
San Francisco

Overcoming Anxiety and Panic interactive guide
© 2019 by Hands-on-Guide, all rights reserved.

Part of the Overcoming Guide series from Hands-on-Guide: www.Overcoming.Guide
Hands-on-Guide
2929 Webster Street
San Francisco, CA 94123 USA
www.handsonguide.com sales@handsonguide.com

ISBN: 978-0-9796408-0-3 paper
Publishing history—first edition, printing 1-01 2019-08
See www.overcoming.guide for corrections and clarifications.

Cover image from iStock.
Cartoon illustrations by Hiraarshad (www.fiverr.com/hiraarshad).
Photo illustration in Figure 10-02 is based on an image from Shutterstock.

Table of Contents

Contents in Brief

Contents in Detail

Preface

I love helping people overcome anxiety or panic because this makes such a positive difference in their lives. For many years I've been using the anxiety model (explained in Chapter 2) to help people understand their anxiety and make changes in their thinking and actions. I have found this approach to be very effective for straightforward anxiety issues and for the anxiety component of more complex psychological problems. I would like to make this approach more widely available.

This guide is the first step in a larger project to help reduce the suffering caused by anxiety in our society that will include:

• Do-it-yourself educational materials to help people overcome anxiety issues on their own, or prepare for therapy, if needed.

• Therapist training resources to help therapists adopt highly effective anxiety treatments, including the therapeutic use of virtual reality technology.

Plans include a series of guides to help with common anxiety-related conditions, such as fears and phobias with therapist guides. For more information, check the website (www.overcoming.guide) and sign-up for our e-mail list.

My goal is to provide a straightforward, understandable guide written with humor, empathy, understanding, and optimism. I want to lead you through the process of understanding your personal anxiety cycle and breaking free of it as quickly as possible.

For many years I have used versions of this guide with clients in individual and group therapy. The experience of working with many different people as they completed the forms and did the exercises helped make this a better book.

Chapter 1

Why You Want This Guide

"I was lost. This is my road map." – Matthew

"I feel better now than I have in many years." – Jennifer

Are you anxious? Have you had an anxiety or panic attack? Do you worry about anxiety or panic attacks?

Does anxiety keep you from doing things you want to do?

Reading this book and completing the forms can help you overcome your anxiety and break free from panic attacks. Overcoming anxiety will help you feel freer and happier. The benefits are long-lasting and do not require medications.

You can use this as a self-help guide for overcoming anxiety on your own or as a workbook while working with a therapist. If you start on your own and find that you are not making progress, consider looking for a therapist who can help you. Information on finding a therapist is provided in the Appendix. Sharing your forms and records with your therapist may help speed-up your improvement.

Does This Really Work?

Yes, this works. I will guide you through a series of steps that will help you learn about anxiety and develop different ways of thinking and acting. These skills incorporate tools from cognitive behavioral therapy (CBT), positive psychology, and other evidence-based techniques with proven effectiveness.

I know these techniques work because–in addition to studying the support-ing research–I have over forty years of professional experience treating panic and anxiety issues. I have helped hundreds of people overcome anxiety by learning and applying these skills.

When someone seeks help for panic attacks or anxiety, I can almost guar-antee that they will be feeling better soon. It is thrilling to see people move from helplessness and fear to freedom and empowerment. I love helping people make this amazing change and wrote this book to share this knowl-edge more widely.

In this book, you will meet people like yourself who were able to overcome anxiety and panic using this six-step approach. Quotations and stories are from people I have helped but the names and identifying details have been changed to protect their privacy.

Here are examples of what clients have said:

> *"I can't believe it! I never thought I would feel this good. I have my life back!"* — *Alyssa*

> *"I was really skeptical at first since I'd had panic attacks for years. Now I'm free and living my life again."* — *Jamie*

> *"I thought it would take years to get through this program. I am amazed at how quickly my panic attacks decreased."* — *Andrew*

> *"My marriage is so much better. We don't argue nearly as much because I'm able to run errands and help out again."* — *Dorothy*

No matter how long you have had panic attacks, no matter how frequent or severe your anxiety, no matter how much anxiety restricts your life, I believe this approach can help you. The people I have helped overcome anxiety in-clude young and old, people from many racial and ethnic backgrounds, cul-tures, and religions, and with all levels of education from doctors to people who never finished high school.

Multiple research studies show that people who practice these skills and follow these suggestions get great results. My client's experience supports this as well. Carlos is a good example (see page 11): after suffering from panic attacks for more than twenty years, Carlos is now enjoying his life, free of anxiety and fear.

If you think "That's great, but it won't work for me." Ask yourself "What have I got to lose by trying?" And then ask yourself "What could I gain if I succeed?" Isn't this worth a try?

I encourage you to give this approach your best shot because *the biggest factor in whether or not people get better seems to be their willingness to do the work.*

Complete the forms and records. Study the information. Apply the ideas. Do the exercises. Practice and use the skills.

Read and re-read this book. Mark it up; underline it; highlight it; memorize it. Think of it as a map showing you the path to a happier, freer life.

This Book Is for You

If you have anxiety or panic attacks that frighten you, this book is for you. If you do what I suggest:

- Panic may stop completely or happen much less often.

- You can experience anxiety or panic calmly, if these sensations occur.

- Fear will no longer limit you, and you will be free to live your life.

- You will learn powerful coping skills and gain increased self-confidence.

This book will help reduce your symptoms and lose your fear by:

- Understanding the anxiety cycle in general and your personal anxiety cycle including your anxiety triggers, fight-or-flight sensations, fear and danger thoughts, and fear-based actions.

- Reducing your anxiety triggers.

- Changing how you respond to the physical sensations of anxiety or panic.

- Thinking differently about fears and danger thoughts; challenging unrealistic fear thoughts and making coping plans for true alarms.

- Acting differently when you experience anxiety or panic sensations and learning that these sensations are safe.

- Engaging in activities that previously caused anxiety and learning that these activities are safe.

How Soon Can You Expect to Feel Better?

Most people with anxiety or panic start feeling better within 2-4 weeks as they complete the first couple of steps. Just reading Chapter 2 or completing the first step (Understanding Your Anxiety Cycle) can be tremendously helpful.

Almost everyone masters these skills in eight weeks or less. If there are many different activities that you avoid because of panic, you may need additional time.

The skills you learn for overcoming anxiety and panic also help decrease fears, worries, phobias, and general anxiety, and can lift your mood. Learning and using these skills creates a positive cycle of change that can spread to other areas of your life.

The more time you invest, the faster change occurs. The more you study this information, complete the forms, and apply the skills, the better you become at handling panic and anxiety attacks.

Forms and Records

Forms and records are important tools in the process of overcoming anxiety. You can use the forms in book and make copies of the Anxiety Record and Panic Record or check the book website for other options: www.overcoming.guide/form-options.

If Reading About Anxiety Scares You

You are not alone if you feel uncomfortable just reading about anxiety or panic attacks. Many people react this way. Here is what you can do:

- Turn to Chapter 2: The Anxiety Cycle for reassuring information. Learn how even the most intense anxiety or panic sensations are harmless and are actually designed to be lifesaving and protective. This information is incredibly reassuring, very calming, and will jumpstart your learning.

As one client said, "After I understood what was going on, I felt so much better. I wasn't as scared, and I was able to read the book without freaking out. The more I read, the better I felt."

Jump ahead right now if you wish. When you are ready, come back here to read and work through the rest of the book.

Are You Feeling Depressed?

Sometimes people who have anxiety or panic also feel depressed. Anxiety and depression can go together in one of three ways:

1. Anxiety can cause depression.
   When you are anxious or panicky, you start to see the world as dangerous. You doubt your ability to cope. You may avoid activities you used to enjoy. You begin to lose self-confidence. Your world shrinks. Life is not much fun. It is easy to get depressed. Overcoming your anxiety can cure your depression.

2. Depression can cause anxiety.
   When you are depressed, your thoughts about everything tend to be negative. If you are flooded with negative thoughts, it is easy to become anxious. If depression came first, treating depression may cure your anxiety.

3. Depression and anxiety can be separate issues that are both present.
   Sometimes you have the stinking bad luck to have two separate conditions at the same time: a depression problem *and* an anxiety problem. Perhaps you know you have a depression problem because you have had prior episodes of depression. Now you are having anxiety or panic and an episode of depression.

Please check to see if you may have depression by completing Form 1-01: Depression Checklist (page 8) based on your feelings over the *last two weeks*.

If you feel like you are in a crisis and are going to hurt yourself or someone else, go to the nearest emergency room or call your local medical emergency number (911 in North America and certain other areas), the National Suicide Prevention Lifeline (1-800-273-8255), or text the Crisis Text Line: in the US text HOME to 741741, in Canada text 686868, in the United Kingdom text 85258.

If you are thinking you want to die, if you are getting more and more depressed all the time, or if you are so depressed you cannot function, contact your health-care provider or a licensed mental health professional and seek treatment

Form 1-01: Depression Checklist

☐ Do you feel generally hopeless about things?

☐ Do you feel sad or depressed most of the time most days?

☐ Do you feel worthless or guilty most of the time?

☐ When things happen you would normally enjoy, do you not enjoy them?

☐ Has your appetite changed so much that you lost or gained weight without trying?

☐ Do you have trouble sleeping, or do you sleep too much?

☐ Do you have much less energy than usual, or do you feel agitated?

☐ Do you wish you could die, or do you think about death or killing yourself?

for depression immediately. See the Appendix for information on finding a therapist.

What to focus on first, depression or anxiety?

If panic and anxiety started <u>before</u> your depression and you are only mildly depressed, try treating your anxiety and panic first. Your mood may return to normal once panic is treated. Of course, if your depression gets worse, or if you are considering suicide, seek help for your depression immediately.

If depression started <u>before</u> your panic, I often recommend treating the depression first. After your mood has improved, come back to this book if you still have—or worry about having—panic symptoms.

Some people treat their depression first, and then their anxiety; others treat anxiety first, then depression; some treat both at the same time. This is up to you. Be aware that depression can make it harder to follow the instructions in this book. If you suspect that this is happening to you, seek treatment for your depression first, and then deal with your panic.

Story: Amanda

Amanda found that her worry about panic was interfering with her life. It limited what she could do and where she went. She realized she was becoming depressed and decided to get help for her anxiety. As she overcame her anxiety and panic, she got her life back, and her depression went away.

There is hope even if you have had anxiety for years

Do not blame yourself for not overcoming panic on your own. The facts about anxiety are not taught in school. If you are like most people, you do not know what to do when you panic.

You may have been too embarrassed to tell anyone. And even if you asked for advice, many well-meaning people make unhelpful suggestions. Here are some examples: "Just relax!", "Don't think about it!", "It's all in your head", or simply, "Nothing is wrong."

You may have thought, "Well, if it's all in my head and nothing's wrong, why does my body feel like this? And exactly how can I *relax* when I'm anxious – tell me that! If I could relax and not think about what makes me anxious, don't you think I would have done that already?!?"

Pretty frustrating, huh? You will not hear any of that from me. In fact, not only will I tell you what to do instead, I will explain why 'just relaxing' or trying to 'not think about it' will not work. Panic is certainly not 'all in your head'; anxiety attacks are very physical.

Introducing Amanda, Raj, Liah, and Carlos

Throughout this book, stories about Amanda, Raj, Liah, and Carlos illustrate different ways in which people overcome anxiety and panic so that you can learn from their mistakes and successes. These stories are based on people I have helped but names and identifying details have been changed to protect their privacy.

Story: Amanda

Amanda is 33 years old, a single mother with two small children. After her divorce, she had to move back in with her parents. While she appreciates her parents' support, living with them is stressful. Amanda works part-time in a small bakery and doesn't make a lot of money. She worries about her future, her children, and whether she will be able to make it on her own.

Amanda's first panic attack happened when she was shopping at the mall with her mother. Amanda remembers it vividly, "We had been in the mall for about an hour when all of a sudden I felt really strange, like I wasn't in my body. I told my mom I needed to sit down because I was dizzy. I felt like I couldn't get a deep breath. I was shaking and felt numb and tingly in my arms and legs. I thought I was dying!"

Amanda's mom got mad at her for "not eating lunch like I told you to," but Amanda didn't think that was the problem. She was sure she was suffocating. "I was really panicked. I told my mom, 'We have to go outside right now and get fresh air before I pass out.'" They went outside, sat for a few minutes, then drove home.

By the time they got home, Amanda felt better, and she was convinced that leaving the mall had saved her life. That was two years ago. She has continued to worry about having another panic attack ever since. She has never gone back to the mall and now she feels uncomfortable in other crowded places. Lately, she has started to feel anxious about going anywhere and she feels like her world is shrinking.

Story: Raj

Raj is a happily married 45-year-old engineer with a son in middle school. He works long hours in a technology start-up and commutes an hour each way in heavy traffic. His long commute and demanding job can be stressful.

Raj had his first panic attack five years ago after getting food poisoning at a big work-related dinner party. Shortly after eating, he started feeling sick to his stomach. He tried to ignore it, but his stomachache worsened. He went home early and began vomiting and having diarrhea. He worried about what might have happened if he had stayed at the party. Ever since then, he starts to panic if he knows he will be in a social setting where he will be expected to eat.

Story: Liah

Liah is a 22-year-old woman who was a straight-A student all through school. She recently graduated from college and started working for a large marketing firm. She loves her job but worries about making mistakes and never feels like she has prepared enough. Because she is eager to succeed and impress her bosses, she spends 50-60 hours a week in the office and takes work home at night and on the weekends.

Liah's anxiety began about 9 months ago, shortly after she started her new job. She panics every Monday morning on her drive to work, anticipating the demands waiting for her at the marketing firm. She has also started waking up during the night in a panic. "It's awful! I feel like I'm not connected to my body. It's like I don't have any control of myself during those times. And why does it happen when I'm asleep?"

Story: Carlos

Carlos is a 67-year-old retired auto mechanic who has worked hard all his life. He helped his parents and his sisters, as well as supporting his own family while his wife stayed home and raised their four sons. Now the sons are married and Carlos and his wife care for three of their nine grandchildren during the day while the parents work. Whenever there is a problem in the family, everybody turns to Carlos.

Carlos has been living with panic and anxiety for over 20 years. Suddenly, with no warning, he gets a fast, racing heartbeat, pressure or pain in his chest, sweating, hot flashes, and a choking sensation in his throat. These are Carlos' *anxiety sensations*.

Carlos' strongest *fear* is that he is having a heart attack. Because of that fear, he has seen many doctors and has had all kinds of medical tests (his *fear-based actions*). In addition to seeing several medical specialists, he has gone to the Emergency Room many times over the years. Doctor after doctor told him "There's nothing wrong with your body." He has become frustrated, angry, and defensive because it seems obvious to him that something *is* wrong, but the doctors can't find it. When his physician recommended that he see a mental health professional, he really resented it. The first thing he said when he came for therapy was "There's nothing wrong with my head, doc. There is something wrong with my body!"

Carlos' experience is common among people with panic and anxiety. When the medical doctors urged him to see a mental health professional, he thought they were trying to get rid of him. Even when his wife urged him to see a therapist, he was reluctant, worrying that the family would be ashamed of him. "I'm a strong person. I take care of everybody. I'm not weak or crazy. This is physical. Talking won't help me."

Getting the Most from This Book

I have been helping people get over having anxiety attacks for many years. It does not seem to matter how frequent or how intense your anxiety or panic symptoms are, or how long you have been having them. What matters most is your commitment to learning and changing. The more time and energy you put into this process, the more benefit you will get from it.

Read and re-read this book. Mark it up. Make it yours. Take the information to heart and practice the tools.

Make a Commitment to Yourself

You are worth the time it takes to break free of anxiety and panic. You deserve to feel better and have your life back. Learning to apply these new skills takes about eight weeks, more for a few people, a lot less for others.

Make a commitment to yourself. Schedule several hours each week for the next eight weeks to read this book and practice the exercises. Plan times in your schedule right now. What days and times will you set aside? Use Form 1-02: Setting Goals to set your target date for being free of anxiety and panic, and the specific days and times when you will work on overcoming anxiety and panic.

Now go put these appointments in your calendar. Remember: you are worth it; make yourself a priority. Make these appointments with yourself—and keep them!

Story: Amanda

Amanda set her alarm to get up an hour earlier on weekday mornings. This gave her quiet time to read and do the exercises before her children woke up.

Form 1-02: Setting Goals

My goal is to overcome anxiety and panic by:

_____

I plan to work on overcoming anxiety and panic during these times:

_____

Story: Raj

Raj blocked out time in his schedule on Mondays and Wednesdays from 7-9 pm. He left work early to make sure he had this time free, turned off his cell phone, and did not check e-mail or try to multi-task during his scheduled time.

Story: Liah

Liah joined a panic therapy group that met weekly. She made a commitment to stop working through her lunch breaks and read this book during that time instead. She did the exercises at home on weekends.

Story: Carlos

Carlos and his wife were busy during the workweek babysitting their grandchildren. By the end of the day, they were happy—but exhausted. They read this book together on the weekends.

Track Your Progress

Later in this book, you will start tracking your progress using Anxiety and Panic Records. Tracking your anxiety or panic attacks, overall anxiety level, and worry about anxiety or panic will help you notice when episodes of anxiety become fewer, shorter, and less severe and your anxiety and worry about anxiety decrease.

Your Panic Records will help you identify important patterns and analyze your personal anxiety cycle. This will let you focus your efforts where they will do the most good, and see results as things improve.

The forms will guide, empower, and encourage you. If you want to start tracking now, see Start Charting (page 108).

Stories: Using the Forms

Amanda kept her forms and this book on her bedside table. That made it easy to update the forms at the end of each day and read the book first thing in the morning.

Liah and Carlos bought notebooks for their forms. Liah liked a small notebook that was easy to carry in her purse and didn't get lost between work, home, and her therapy group. "It really helped me keep track of what I was learning."

Carlos said having the forms in his notebook made it easy to see his progress. "Whenever I got discouraged, I could look back and see how much better I was and how much progress I had made. That kept me going."

At first, Raj did not use the forms to track progress and patterns. He was busy and filling out forms felt "like a waste of time". He was embarrassed to fill out a Panic Record around other people and did not want to excuse himself for a few minutes. He would promise himself he'd fill out the form later, but somehow "I never found time."

Several weeks into therapy, Raj was not getting better as we would have expected. He realized that he was only going to get out of treatment as much as he put into it. He started doing the forms on his phone and filling out Panic Records as soon as he could when he had panic sensations. "I realized I had to make this a priority."

Completing the forms helped Raj identify patterns in his thoughts and actions. This information helped him make changes, and he began seeing improvement. He told us, "The best advice I can give someone is to keep the records. Believe me, it is worth the trouble."

The people who get better the fastest and make the most progress, are those who devote the most time and effort to changing. I encourage you to do

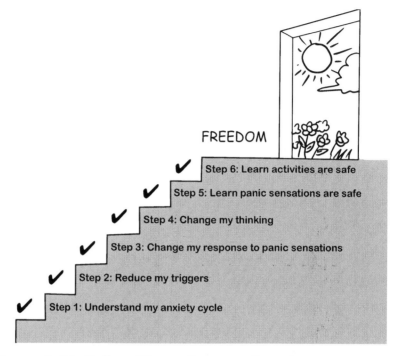

FREEDOM

✔ Step 6: Learn activities are safe

✔ Step 5: Learn panic sensations are safe

✔ Step 4: Change my thinking

✔ Step 3: Change my response to panic sensations

✔ Step 2: Reduce my triggers

✔ Step 1: Understand my anxiety cycle

Figure 1-01: Follow These Steps to Freedom

everything suggested in this book. Each recommended action is included because other people with panic have found that it helped.

Reward Yourself

Reward and praise yourself for completing each step. Notice how your efforts contribute to your progress. Praise yourself for buying and reading this book. Do something enjoyable every time you finish a chapter, fill out a form, or complete an exercise.

Use Form 1-03: Rewards Plan (page 16) to give yourself incentives for completing each of the six steps in this book.

Focus on the Positive

Compare your ratings over time as you progress through the book. Focus on positive changes and keep going. Overcoming anxiety and panic is your goal; this book is your path to that goal.

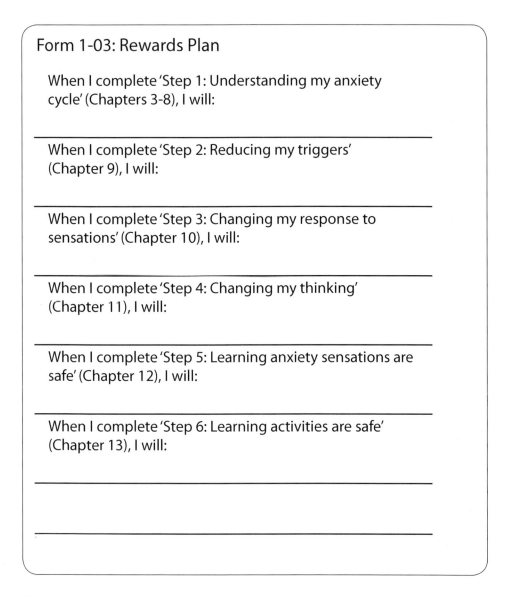

Form 1-03: Rewards Plan

When I complete 'Step 1: Understanding my anxiety cycle' (Chapters 3-8), I will:

_____

When I complete 'Step 2: Reducing my triggers' (Chapter 9), I will:

_____

When I complete 'Step 3: Changing my response to sensations' (Chapter 10), I will:

_____

When I complete 'Step 4: Changing my thinking' (Chapter 11), I will:

_____

When I complete 'Step 5: Learning anxiety sensations are safe' (Chapter 12), I will:

_____

When I complete 'Step 6: Learning activities are safe' (Chapter 13), I will:

_____

_____

Think of each form, each exercise, and each change, as one step along that path. You only need to take one step at a time. Just keep taking the next small step and you will reach your goal.

Neither the number of steps, nor the size of each step, matters. What matters is taking the next step, whatever it is–and continuing to take the next step—one step after another, until you are free of anxiety and panic.

Keep moving forward. Panic can only defeat you if *you stop*. I have seen people free themselves from panic who had trouble even leaving the house before learning how to overcome their anxiety. They did it and you can do it too.

Getting Help

Some people find it is easier and faster to work through this process with help from a therapist, friends, or family. Consider looking for professional help if you:

• Have trouble starting the process described here.

• Feel stuck, like you are not making progress, or are going around in circles.

• Marked several items on Form 1-01: Depression Checklist (page 8) and feel that depression may be making it hard for you to work on anxiety and panic.

• Have other reasons why you think help from a therapist would be beneficial.

See the Appendix for information on finding a therapist.

Friends and Family

It helps to have someone who can remind you of the facts if you panic and can encourage you to use the new skills you are learning. Pick people you trust and with whom you feel comfortable. Your helpers should make you feel better, not worse or more anxious. At the same time, overcoming panic means facing your fears. You *do want* people who will encourage you to change.

Find people who will praise your efforts, congratulate you on your progress, and celebrate your successes. You may want to have your helping friend or family member read this book so they share your new knowledge about panic and can support you as you complete the forms and do the exercises.

Share your goals on Form 1-02: Setting Goals (page 13) and your plans for rewarding yourself on Form 1-03: Rewards Plan (page 16) with your friends and family so they can help you meet your goals and remind you of planned rewards if you get discouraged.

Unhelpful

Try to avoid talking about your anxiety with people who become angry or critical. Sometimes well-meaning, caring people give unhelpful advice because of their own anxiety or because they are misinformed. Do not let others encourage you to run away or avoid. You do not want to involve people who will increase your fears.

Helpers can lovingly encourage you to push yourself. Seek out people who will support your freedom, not your fear. Your fear does not need helpers!

Story: Amanda

Amanda tried to do the program on her own at first, but after a couple of weeks, she asked a friend for help. Together, they read this book and learned about panic. "It was such a relief to stop trying to hide my anxiety. And my friend would encourage me whenever I felt down or scared." Amanda made more progress, and their friendship became stronger.

Story: Carlos

Carlos felt better after he included his wife in his efforts. Even though he had been having panic attacks for years, he and his wife learned a lot of new information and coping skills that helped them both. She was able to remind him about the facts whenever he would worry that something was medically wrong. Over time, Carlos told several family members and was surprised to learn that two of his children had anxiety as well. It felt good to share what he had learned and to help his children overcome their anxiety.

Keep in Touch

Please keep in touch, even if you get what you need without reading the entire book.

If you find this helpful, please tell your friends and family, post reviews on Amazon.com or similar websites, and share this book on Facebook. Also let me know (via Overcoming.guide) if you see ways to improve this material.

Chapter 2

The Anxiety Cycle

"Understanding my anxiety cycle gives me a clear picture of what is going on. Now I know I'm not crazy." – Michael

Although an anxiety or panic attack can happen very quickly, anxiety is actually a cycle with four parts. Identifying the elements of your personal anxiety cycle will help you understand and overcome anxiety and panic.

Understanding the Anxiety Cycle

The anxiety cycle has four parts as shown in Figure 2-01 (page 20): Anxiety Triggers, Fight-or-Flight Sensations, Fear and Danger Thoughts, and Fear-Based Actions.

Anxiety triggers send messages of threat to a primitive part of the brain we call the Reacting Brain. You will learn all about the Reacting Brain below.

Examples of anxiety triggers include chemical factors, external stresses, self-talk including unrealistic self-demands, unhelpful lessons learned from past events, and situations your primitive brain associates with danger. Some people have genetic triggers or inherited factors that make their nervous system more prone to panic.

Identifying your personal anxiety triggers helps explain when and why you experience anxiety or panic attacks. Triggers can even explain panic attacks that seem to come out of nowhere, such as panic while you are relaxing or sleeping, as we discuss later.

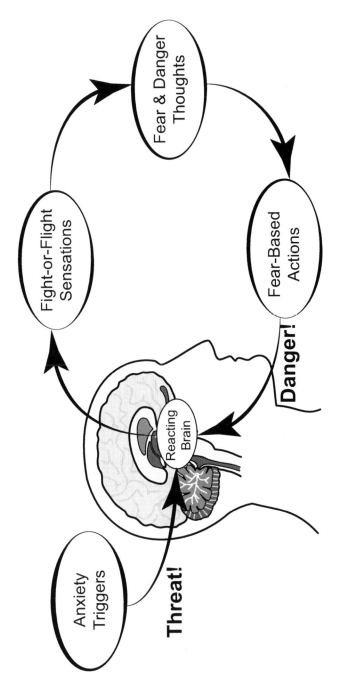

Figure 2-01: Anxiety Cycle Overview

Fight-or-flight sensations associated with anxiety or panic are feelings within your body triggered by adrenaline and other neurotransmitters that your brain releases in response to a perceived threat. Sensations may include fast heartbeat, shortness of breath, dizziness, shaking, and other physical reactions we will cover later.

Fear and danger thoughts are all the thoughts and images that come to mind when you feel anxious or panicky. These can include fears, worries, anxious thoughts, dire predictions, negative assumptions, and false conclusions about what is happening or will happen. Fears are learned and can be changed by new experiences, insights, logic, and knowledge. The more you can put your fears into words, the better you can question and challenge them. You may already know your fears, or you may have to figure them out.

Fear-based actions are everything you do—or avoid doing—because of your anxiety or panic sensations, fears, and danger thoughts. Fear-based actions are motivated by fear, panic, or worry.

Anxiety triggers, sensations, fear and danger thoughts, and fear-based actions create a vicious cycle of anxiety and panic that feeds on itself over time, creating more triggers, more panic reactions, more fear thoughts, and more fear-based actions or avoidance. The more you understand your personal anxiety cycle, the more quickly you can change it.

Introducing Your Brain

Your amazing brain has evolved over millions of years and includes specialized areas for many different tasks. We'll focus on the two parts of the brain most involved in creating—and overcoming—panic.

Your Two Brains

In many ways, your brain is really two brains in one as shown in Figure 2-02 Reacting Brain and Thinking Brain (page 22). Your Reacting Brain includes primitive lower parts of the brain (the amygdala and hippocampus) that react quickly and automatically to possible threats. This part of our brains is essentially unchanged since caveman days.

Messages of threat go directly to your caveman Reacting Brain and it does precisely what its name says: it reacts. It is not verbal or conscious. It does not stop to think; it reacts. When it gets a message about any kind of threat,

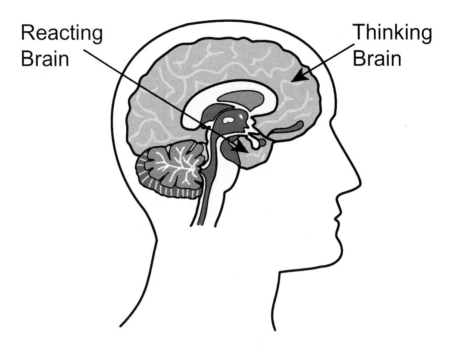

Reacting Brain

Thinking Brain

Figure 2-02: Reacting Brain and Thinking Brain

it immediately triggers a rush of physical changes to prepare you to fight or run. This is the "fight-or-flight" response.

Your Thinking Brain is the more highly evolved brain area (cerebral cortex) that makes us fully human. The Thinking Brain is verbal and conscious. It is larger, more developed, and smarter—but slower—than your Reacting Brain. The Thinking Brain is capable of the rational thought and logical judgment: it thinks.

> *"Emotions can, and often do, begin very quickly, so quickly, in fact, that our conscious self does not participate in or even witness what in our mind triggers an emotion at any particular moment. That speed can save our lives in an emergency, but it can also ruin our lives when we overreact."* — *Paul Ekman, PhD*

When you panic, it may feel as if there's an argument going on between two parts of your brain. One part is screaming, "Panic! Threat! Danger! Run!",

Figure 2-03: Thinking Brain and 'Caveman' Reacting Brain

while the other is yelling, "Stop it! Shut up! Calm down!" This is because there **is** an argument going on between two parts of your brain.

I will teach you how to help your Thinking Brain win these arguments.

Your Reacting Brain Bodyguard

Humans used to live in a world filled with dangerous predators. Thousands of years ago, people faced daily threats of animal attack. If a hungry lion attacked, you had to instantly run fast or fight hard to survive—otherwise you were lion lunch.

Humans have no fangs, no claws, no hard-protective shell. To predators, people must have looked like walking shish kebobs!

The Reacting Brain allowed your ancestors to survive in that dangerous world and so this part of the brain was passed down pretty much unchanged through the ages. Your Reacting Brain today is automatic, primitive, and left over from caveman days when the dangers were physical, attacks were unpredictable, and a fast, unthinking response would save your life.

Your Reacting Brain does not stop and think. It reacts—with an intense, physical, life-saving, harmless, protective physical response designed to help you run or fight, so you survive.

If you have to run, it wants you to run as fast as possible to reach safety. If you have to fight, it wants you to survive a life-and-death struggle.

You are here today because of your ancestors' strong Reacting Brain. It protected your ancestors by automatically noticing potential threats, instantly reacting to them, and then remembering everything associated with threat or danger.

Always on Guard

Your Reacting Brain's job is to keep you alive. It is in charge of many essential functions that happen without conscious thought or awareness. This includes things like regulating your body temperature, blood pressure, heart rate, and breathing.

Your Reacting Brain is awake, aware, and protecting you 24 hours a day, 7 days a week, whether you are awake or asleep, paying attention or not. Your Reacting Brain constantly works to keep you alive and safe by scanning both your body and your environment for signs of possible danger and by reacting to what it thinks might be potential threats.

Caveman Brain in a Modern World

Your Reacting Brain is devoted to your safety. Just like your personal bodyguard or Secret Service agent, it is constantly searching for threat or danger. This is a good thing when you are in actual physical danger.

The problem is that the world in which you live has changed, but your brain has not kept up. Most of the time, you are not in physical danger. You rarely fight mountain lions or run to escape falling objects. The "threats" you face in the modern world are likely to be emotional or financial, rather than physical.

Even though you live in a modern world with different threats, this part of your brain is still a caveman's brain. Your Reacting Brain has one – *and only one* – response to any kind of threat: the fight-or-flight response. This is true whether the threat is real or imaginary, physical or financial, remembered from the past, or created within your mind as you think about your future.

Real and Imagined Threats

Information goes to your Reacting Brain first—before your Thinking Brain—and reactions happen without time-consuming analysis. For example, if you are watching a 3D movie, your Reacting Brain may react to an object that appears to be flying toward your face before your Thinking Brain can identify it as an imaginary and harmless 3D baseball. This, by the way, is why facing feared situations in a simulated virtual reality environment can be a powerful tool for therapy.

Facing feared activities or situations in a 3-dimensional, immersive virtual reality environment is a powerful tool in overcoming fears when used along with the approach described in this book. Using virtual reality in this way is often called Virtual Reality Therapy or Virtual Reality Exposure Therapy (see Find a therapist offering Virtual Reality Therapy on page 250).

Your Reacting Brain is not able to distinguish between messages of threat generated by *real*, physical danger from the outside world and messages of "threat" created by words, mental pictures, past memories, or worries about the future.

Your Reacting Brain learns from experience, both your personal experiences and other people's experiences. It not only reacts to things that have happened to you, it also reacts to and learns from things that happen to other people as well as things that happen on television or in movies. This explains why, after the September 11 attacks on the World Trade Center, people in California who saw the attacks on television suddenly became more aware of, and frightened by, the sight and sound of airplanes although they had not personally experienced the attacks.

Devoted, but Dumb

Your caveman, bodyguard Reacting Brain takes every message of threat seriously. As a result, this devoted, but dumb, protector can cause real problems for you.

Because your Reacting Brain's job is to protect you, it learns danger very quickly and remembers everything associated with the situation. It never really forgets a danger. In fact, once it believes something is a threat, it not only reacts when you encounter it again, it also easily decides that anything and everything it associated with this threatening situation or experience is dangerous. This includes things like where you were, who you were with, or what you were doing, feeling, or thinking at the time. Anything the Reacting Brain connects with danger can become an anxiety trigger.

So, for example, let's say your heart was pounding after you narrowly avoided hitting a pedestrian while driving on a rainy night. Your overly protective Reacting Brain might decide that a rapid heartbeat is dangerous, that driving in the rain or at night is dangerous, or that driving itself or even being a passenger is dangerous.

Left on its own, it can become more and more likely to leap into action and start trying to "save you" from "dangers" that do not exist. In other words, your Reacting Brain triggers panic attacks.

If you do not understand what is happening when your Reacting Brain needlessly triggers a panic attack, it can be very frightening. Understanding the Reacting Brain dramatically reduces fear of panic.

Your Reacting Brain in Review

Your caveman Reacting Brain:

- Is a life-saving bodyguard that reacts quickly to perceived threats.

- Controls many important bodily functions.

- Is primitive and automatic, so it may react unnecessarily and send false alarms.

- Learns quickly and—right or wrong—remembers every experience it associates with threat, danger, or fear.

- May react in response to threats that only exist in your imagination, to memories from the past, to what you think may happen in the future, to unhelpful lessons from the past, or to your worries.

- Reacts to all threats by preparing you to run or fight in order to survive by releasing adrenaline.

- Triggers a physical fight-or-flight response that is natural and safe even though it may include intense or uncomfortable sensations.

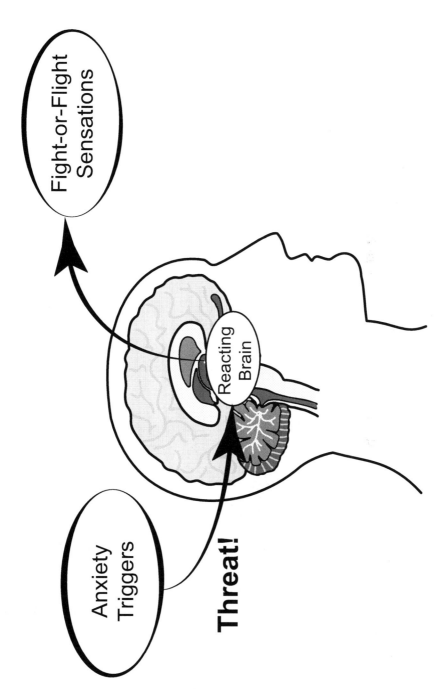

Figure 2-04: Anxiety Leading to Fight-or-Flight Sensations

Figure 2-05: Reacting Brain is faster than the Thinking Brain

Your Thinking Brain

The good news is that the Reacting Brain is only a small part of your brain. You have a much larger, more developed, and smarter area of your brain that makes you fully human: your Thinking Brain.

This part of your brain helps you think consciously and logically. Your Thinking Brain helps you analyze facts and make deliberate decisions. It is verbal and can learn through words and logic.

Smarter, but Slower

Your Thinking Brain is smarter than your Reacting Brain. It is bigger and more powerful in many ways. BUT—here's the problem—it is s-l-o-w-e-r.

Your Thinking Brain and Reacting Brain are connected and share information, but "threat" messages reach your Reacting Brain first.

You now know what your Reacting Brain does in response to threat messages: it reacts, immediately and physically. It instantly jumps into action to save you from danger, yelling "Threat! Danger! Run for your life!"

Shortly afterward, your Thinking Brain comes along and says, "Now wait just a minute. Hold on. Let's take a look at what's actually happening." Unfortunately, by then your panic anxiety response has already been activated.

Using Your Thinking Brain

I will teach you how to help your Thinking Brain re-program and override your Reacting Brain, helping it to learn when you are *not* in danger. You will learn to respond to triggers in ways that make your situation better, not worse.

Panic is the Fight-or-Flight Response

When your Reacting Brain thinks you face a threat, it triggers the release of adrenaline. Adrenaline is a stress hormone that prepares the body for action by activating the sympathetic nervous system. Think of the "s" in sympathetic as meaning "Save your life" or "Stress response." Sympathetic nervous system arousal is the "Fight-or-Flight Response."

In a panic attack, sympathetic nervous system arousal prepares your body to fight or run—even though there is no actual danger. Among other things, it increases your heart rate and breathing, releases stored energy, and slows down digestion. It creates the physical sensations associated with panic.

"I'll Save You!"

Every bodily change that happens during panic has an intended life-saving, protective purpose. Your body is designed to respond in this way, and is built to handle this response.

The bodily changes of panic help save your life when you are truly in danger. Let's look at a modern-day example. You are crossing the street when suddenly, out of the corner of your eye, you notice a car running a red light and racing toward you. Without stopping to think, you automatically jump out of the car's path.

Fight, Flight, or Freeze?

The "Fight-or-Flight" response is sometimes called the "Fight, Flight, or Freeze" response. Some people hear "freeze" and think panic can paralyze a person and make them unable to move. This is *NOT* true.

In response to threat, adrenaline is released to prepare your body to act and the Reacting Brain tenses your muscles in preparation to run or fight. Your muscles may feel very tight, but you can still move them.

When you feel helpless or don't know what is happening, sometimes the best option may be to "freeze" and wait until you understand what is happening and see a clear opportunity to act. You could think of this as the "deer in the headlights" response.

If you are frightened by or concerned about anxiety sensations, emotions, or fear thoughts, you will be more likely to feel helpless and uncertain. As you learn more about anxiety, you will feel less frightened by panic and will be better prepared to respond in appropriate and helpful ways.

Having narrowly escaped death, you stand on the curb panting as you watch the car speed away. Your heart is pounding a mile a minute, your hands are shaking, your entire body feels tense and trembling at the same time. Adrenaline is rushing through your system and you can still feel the fear.

Despite these intense physical and emotional reactions, you do not say, "Call an ambulance! Something is medically wrong" or "I'm going crazy." No, you say, "Did you see that idiot?! He almost KILLED ME!"

Your body's reaction makes sense to you. You understand why it happened. It saved your life—as it is designed to do.

A panic attack is the very same reaction; you just don't understand why it is happening. In a panic attack, your anxiety triggers cause your Reacting Brain to set off the fight-or-flight response unnecessarily. Your brain sends a false alarm and acts to "save you" from "a danger" that does not exist.

Figure 2-06: Saved by the Reacting Brain

Your panic attack is the very same reaction that saved your life in the example above. It is just responding to a false alarm.

Take a moment and think about that. If the fight-or-flight response is safe for you to experience when you need it, then it is safe for you to experience when you don't need it. If it is safe, it is safe—whether or not you understand what triggered it.

Although it is uncomfortable and unpleasant when it fires off needlessly, panic is the same fight-or-flight response that saves your life. It makes no sense that a life-saving response to danger would make you drop dead, pass out, go crazy, or be unable to function. Any ancestor with a response to danger that made them drop dead, pass out, go crazy, or be unable to function would not have survived to pass on that nervous system to their descendants. Your Reacting Brain, although frustratingly stupid at times, has been shaped by surviving thousands of years of threat and danger.

Answers to Common Questions

What is anxiety?

Anxiety is a broad term. Panic attacks are one type of anxiety problem, but anxiety can also show up as excessive worrying, nervousness, tension, post-traumatic stress symptoms, obsessive-compulsive behaviors, fears, phobias, and in other ways.

In this book, I focus on helping you understand and overcome anxiety that causes anxiety attacks, panic attacks, panic disorder, and/or agoraphobia. You may be puzzled by what these terms mean, so let's explain them:

Anxiety attack and panic attack are two terms for the same experience: a rush of fear associated with sudden changes in your body. A panic attack (or anxiety attack) is officially defined as an experience of intense fear or discomfort that starts quickly, usually peaks within 10 minutes, and includes four or more of these symptoms: rapid heartbeat, sweating, trembling or shaking, feeling short of breath, a tight throat or feeling of choking, chest pain or discomfort, nausea or stomach distress, feeling dizzy or unsteady or faint, numbness or tingling, feeling hot or cold, feeling as if you are not present or as if things are not real, fear that you are losing control or going crazy, and/or fearing you are dying.

Panic disorder is when you have had two or more panic attacks that seem to come out of the blue and you worry about having another panic attack or you have changed what you do out of fear of the attacks.

Agoraphobia is when you are avoiding situations or activities out of fear of having another panic attack. Your fear of panic leads you to change what you do in ways that interfere with your life.

It is easy to have anxiety about anxiety or panic attacks. Unpredictable panic can leave you frightened and worried. Even one or two anxiety-related sensations can be scary and distressing. This book can help.

Do other people have anxiety or panic attacks?

Anxiety and panic attacks are *very common*. According to a telephone survey of the general population, one out of every three people experienced a panic attack within the last year. Anxiety can start in childhood and affects people of all ages. In recent years anxiety appears to be affecting more people.

How do anxiety and sleep affect each other?

You probably know that anxiety can interfere with sleep. Anxiety or worry can make it hard to go to sleep. Panic attacks may wake you in the middle of the night. What you may not know is that sleeping less than 7-9 hours per night or low-quality sleep can increase anxiety. Signs of poor sleep quality include not feeling rested even after getting enough sleep, waking repeatedly during the night, and snoring or gasping for air.

Research shows that inadequate or interrupted sleep can make anxiety or panic more likely and can interfere with learning. Brain scans of sleep-deprived people show a 60% increase in emotional reactivity within the Reacting Brain (amygdala).

If you routinely sleep fewer than 7 hours per night or your sleep is interrupted, impaired sleep may be increasing your anxiety and making it harder for you to learn new ways of dealing with anxiety. Sleeping pills such as Ambien (Zolpidem), Lunesta (Eszopiclone), Belsomra (Suvorexant), etc. can also interfere with learning.

If sleep is a problem, start by making sleep a priority. Stick to a regular sleep schedule. Follow good sleep hygiene. If you have trouble getting to sleep or staying asleep, ask your health care provider about any medical issues (such as sleep apnea) or medications that may be interfering with your sleep.

Working on overcoming anxiety and making sleep a priority can help you feel better. If insomnia is a persistent problem, cognitive behavioral therapy for insomnia (CBT-I) is the recommended treatment. For more information see: www.nhlbi.nih.gov/health-topics/all-publications-and-resources/your-guide-healthy-sleep.

Is panic caused by a disease?

While it is a good idea to have a medical check-up to rule out illnesses that can cause anxiety symptoms, like thyroid disease, illness is not a common cause of anxiety and panic. Panic attacks caused by disease are very rare.

In fact, the ability to have sensations of anxiety or panic generally means your nervous system is healthy and functioning normally. *The problem is your healthy anxiety response is being triggered when it is not needed.*

When your body starts doing unexpected things (like heart racing, feeling faint, sweating, or shaking), most people go to the doctor. Often by the time people see a psychotherapist, they have been to doctors, had tests, and perhaps made several trips to the emergency room. It is frustrating when doctors say, "Everything is fine" but your body does not *feel* fine.

Chapter 3: Your Anxiety Triggers explains why and how the panic response can misfire. If you want to learn more about this right away, skip ahead and read that section now.

Did your anxiety begin shortly after you started or stopped a medication, supplement, or street drug, or shortly after you increased or decreased the dose of a drug? If this is the case, ask your healthcare provider if this could be the cause of your anxiety. Chemicals that can trigger anxiety are discussed later, see Chemical Triggers (page 44).

Do I have a chemical imbalance?

Sometimes people are told their panic attacks are due to a "chemical imbalance." While it *is true* that anxiety can run in families, many people, including people with a family history of anxiety, have overcome panic without medication by following a program such as this one.

In Chapter 3: Your Anxiety Triggers, we review many different things that can trigger panic and anxiety, including heredity and genetic factors. If anxiety or depression run in your family, you may be more vulnerable to panic. That *does not* mean you have a chemical imbalance or that you need medication for panic. It *does* mean you want to understand panic and respond skillfully and effectively.

Do I need anti-anxiety medicine?

My experience—and the research evidence—shows that most people get the best results from treating anxiety and fear of panic attacks *without medicine.* Since some doctors think differently, let me explain my thinking.

Research

First, a very large, well-designed research study on panic treatments found that while people taking medicine initially got faster symptom relief, they did *less well in the long term.* Those treated with medication had more ongoing fear of panic and their panic attacks were more likely to return after they stopped the medicine. Other studies also show that relapse and return of fears are more likely if medication is the only treatment.

Second, the generally recommended "best practice" treatment for panic disorder is the cognitive behavioral therapy for anxiety and panic similar to the approach outlined here.

Third, some medications—such as short-acting anti-anxiety medications—can contribute to panic disorder by causing rebound anxiety or interfere with learning how to overcome panic disorder.

Pros and Cons

Medicines, especially fast-acting anti-anxiety medications (also called tranquilizers or benzodiazepines) like Xanax (Alprazolam), Ativan (Lorazepam), Klonopin (Clonazepam), and others, are often prescribed. They can *stop* the physical sensations of anxiety or panic.

However, there are many disadvantages to relying on medicine alone. One major disadvantage is that tranquilizers can be addicting. A second disadvantage is that these medicines only reduce sympathetic nervous system arousal temporarily. They do not change the rest of your anxiety cycle. Your anxiety triggers are not reduced by taking a pill. Fears about panic remain and may even get worse because you feel like you need to take a pill to stop the sensations. The action of taking a pill to stop panic sensations because they frighten you is a fear-based action. Fear-based actions make your Reacting Brain even more convinced that panic and everything associated with it is dangerous.

Boiling Over

A panic attack is a little like a pot of water that is boiling over because it is sitting on the stove with the heat on under it. Taking a fast-acting anti-anxiety pill is like adding a little cool water to the pot. It stops the water boiling for a moment, but it doesn't turn down the heat and it doesn't move the pot. Nothing has really changed. The water is going to be boiling again soon.

What you really want is to turn down the flame and/or move the pot! The suggestions in this book will help you do that.

Can Medicine Help with Other Anxiety Issues?

In my experience, medicine *can* be very helpful for anxiety problems *other* than panic disorder. For example, people with generalized anxiety disorder (where you over-worry about everything all day for months or years), post-traumatic stress disorder (PTSD), social anxiety disorder, or obsessive-compulsive disorder (OCD) often benefit from medication combined with specific cognitive behavioral therapy (CBT) or other proven therapies for these conditions.

If you are reading this book to get over panic attacks, this approach should give you good, lasting results without medicine. If you have additional anxiety problems or other issues, you may want to discuss treatment options with your therapist (if you have one) and/or your healthcare provider in order to make the best choice for your unique situation.

Can I stop my medicine?

If you are taking medicine for anxiety or panic and want to stop, talk your healthcare provider before stopping. I advise you **not to stop** any medication suddenly because some medicines can have serious withdrawal effects.

A program like this, that gives you other coping skills, is particularly helpful if you want to decrease or stop anti-anxiety medications. Check with your healthcare provider and work out a plan for changing or tapering off your medications based on your specific needs and situation.

What if I have a medical problem?

I have successfully treated many people for panic who also have medical conditions. People with diabetes, hypertension (high blood pressure), asthma, mitral valve prolapse, chronic pain, and other medical conditions have all lost their fear of panic. Even heart attack survivors have been able to carry out this program and successfully overcome panic.

Chapter Summary

Congratulations, you have completed this chapter and covered important information about how the anxiety cycle works, your two brains, where panic comes from, and the purpose of panic. We also covered common questions about anxiety and panic.

Track your progress on Form 2-99: Completed Chapter 2. Note things you have learned, or been surprised by, in this chapter.

Form 2-99: Completed Chapter 2

Date completed: _____

Lessons learned:

_____

Step 1 Understanding Your Anxiety Cycle

"When I didn't know what was happening to me, I was really scared."
– Sandy

"Understanding how anxiety works was huge." – Karen

"Understanding the symptoms and what was going on in my body was very profound. I felt better right away. I would tell myself, 'it's just panic'." – Shelley

The good news about anxiety is that we understand how it works. We know what tends to trigger anxiety and what tends to maintain or worsen it, creating a vicious cycle, whether anxiety is expressed as worry, nervousness, or panic attacks. This is true even for panic attacks that seem to come 'out of the blue' for no reason. In this section, you learn about your personal anxiety cycle and understand what happens when you panic. This includes your specific triggers, sensations, fear and danger thoughts, and fear-based actions.

In the next section, you start using what you learned to break your anxiety cycle.

Your Anxiety Triggers

"Understanding my panic triggers made the anxiety attacks less scary. I realized that there were actually reasons I was panicking." – Sarah

This chapter helps you identify your anxiety triggers. Knowing your triggers helps you make sense of what is happening, suggests ways to reduce anxiety triggers, and reassures you that you are not crazy or out of control.

Panic can be especially frightening when it seems to come out of the blue without a clear trigger, as I explain in the next chapter. Being afraid when you are in real danger is useful and makes perfect sense. It is hard to understand why you panic when there is *no* real danger.

Understanding your panic triggers is part of Step 1 in solving the puzzle of panic and breaking your cycle of fear and anxiety. Completing the checklists and forms in this chapter will help you understand your personal anxiety cycle, identify patterns, and make changes leading to positive results.

Five factors tend to trigger the anxiety response, even when you are not being threatened or facing danger. These triggers can result in panic in the absence of actual danger:

- Genetic factors

- Chemicals

- External Stress

- Self-talk, including Unrealistic Self-Demands

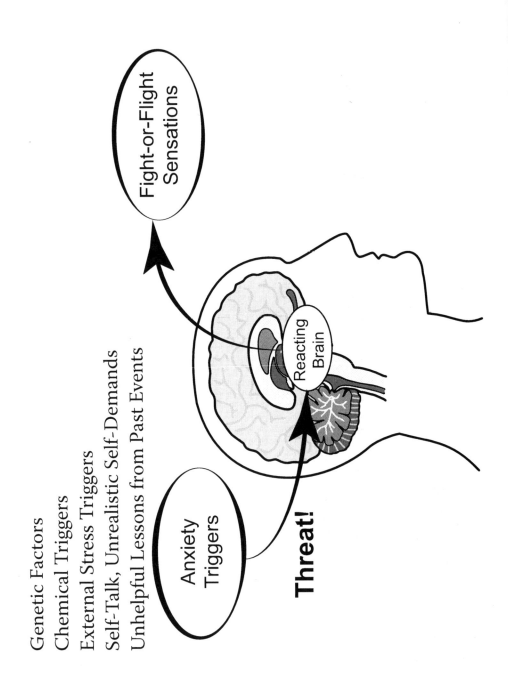

Figure 3-01: Anxiety Triggers

- Unhelpful Lessons from Past Events

Genetic Factors

A tendency to anxiety can run in families. Genetic factors can make some people more likely to have fears, worries, or panic attacks. People with this inherited tendency may *also* be more likely to have depression or problems with alcohol or drug abuse. If your blood relatives have any of these problems, it may be a sign that your nervous system tends to react more quickly or intensely than other people's.

Story: Amanda

Amanda knew that her mother had struggled with anxiety and depression for most of her life, but Amanda had not known that her other relatives had similar issues. After learning that anxiety can run in families, Amanda talked with her mom. She found out that her grandmother had been anxious and tended to worry, two of her uncles had alcohol problems, and a cousin was being treated for panic attacks and depression.

Amanda realized that she might have a genetic trigger making her more vulnerable to panic. This really motivated her to learn how to deal with panic.

Story: Liah

Liah also had genetic factors that made her more likely to have anxiety and depression. When Liah was a young girl, her mother was hospitalized because of significant depression and anxiety. Liah was relieved when she learned that her symptoms weren't "all my fault" but might be partly due to her genes. This allowed Liah to accept herself more and to actively learn new skills for coping with anxiety.

Do You have Genetic Factors?

Think about your blood relatives. This includes your extended family: biological parents and grandparents, aunts and uncles, nieces, nephews, and cousins, brothers and sisters, and children. It does *not* include in-laws, stepparents, or adopted family members. Record your answers on Form 3-01: Relatives with Anxiety (page 45).

The more relatives you have with these issues, the more likely that inherited genetic factors contribute to your anxiety and make you more reactive to other anxiety triggers.

Chemical Triggers

Certain chemicals make panic more likely. These include caffeine and other legal stimulants, alcohol, tobacco, marijuana (especially edibles), many illegal drugs, some medications, and female hormone changes.

Caffeine and Other Legal Stimulants

Legal stimulants include caffeine, nicotine, ephedrine, guarana, hoodia, ginseng, etc. Stimulants are found in coffee drinks, teas (including some herbal teas), some sodas, "energy drinks," "sports drinks," some foods, food products such as "energy bars," and many cold medications. Venti and other super-sized beverages may contain larger amounts of stimulant.

Stimulants do not create panic, but they *can* cause panic-like physical sensations such as a rapid heartbeat (palpitations), trembling, shakiness, and feeling edgy or jittery.

Stimulants make panic more likely in two ways. First, if you are already revved up by a stimulant, panic is more easily triggered. Second, if you fear anxiety or panic sensations, anything that creates a similar feeling can trigger a panic attack.

Alcohol

Alcohol has two different effects on anxiety. The first effect of drinking is that you feel more relaxed. The second effect of drinking is the opposite: alcohol makes you more likely to have anxiety for up to two days afterward. Alcohol also increases stress by interfering with deep restorative sleep.

For these reasons, be cautious about drinking alcohol. It may be tempting to drink to relax, but you run a high risk of alcohol problems if you drink to cope with anxiety. In particular, people who feel anxious in social situations and drink to relax have high rates of alcoholism. Using the skills in this book to cope with anxiety is a much better approach.

Form 3-01: Relatives with Anxiety

Enter the number of your blood relatives who have or used to have:

_____ Panic or anxiety attacks

_____ Unrealistic fears

_____ Excessive worry

Need to do things in a rigid, special way such as repeated hand washing, excessive checking or repeating, unnecessary cleaning, etc.

_____ Significant depression

_____ An alcohol or drug problem

Smoking

Some research suggests that the more you smoke the more anxiety you develop over time. Vaping (Juul or similar products) seems to promote anxiety in ways that are similar to tobacco. Former smokers have reported that they are calmer, sleep better, and their hands are steadier after quitting smoking. Because nicotine is addicting, it can cause withdrawal symptoms–including anxiety. Tobacco temporarily relieves the withdrawal/anxiety symptoms but increases your addiction, strengthening another vicious cycle.

Marijuana

Marijuana, cannabis, THC, hashish, or synthetic cannabinoids (K2, Spice), can trigger panic attacks, even though marijuana is legal or available by prescription in some areas. Some people had their first, or worst, panic attack while smoking marijuana or after eating cannabis edibles. Edibles are especially likely to trigger panic because it is hard to know how much you have ingested, and the effect can be delayed and then hit you hard.

CBD (cannabidiol) is a chemical compound found in cannabis and hemp. CBD supplements are being promoted to treat many conditions including anxiety. However, there has been very little research on CBD for anxiety.

While CBD may relieve some anxiety symptoms—like anti-anxiety medications—there is no evidence of repeated use leading to long-term benefits. See Do I need anti-anxiety medicine (page 34).

In the US and many other countries, non-prescription CBD products are not subject to production guidelines or mandatory lab testing. Consequently, products may contain varying amounts of CBD and may also contain other cannabinoid compounds, including anxiety-promoting THC.

Street Drugs

Many street drugs can cause anxiety or panic, especially drugs like cocaine (coke, crack), hallucinogens, inhalants, MDMA (Ecstasy), methamphetamines (meth, speed, crank), PCP, and misuse of prescription medications. Drug withdrawal can also cause anxiety.

Over-the-Counter Drugs and Supplements

Many non-prescription drugs, herbal remedies, and dietary supplements can increase anxiety or panic attacks, especially those that contain caffeine, ephedra, or other stimulating compounds. Examples are cold remedies, decongestants, energy boosters, and weight loss products. Some supplements for body building or weight loss contain anabolic steroids and similar compounds that can cause panic attacks.

Prescription Medications

Some prescription medications can cause jitteriness, racing heart, shaking, insomnia or other anxiety symptoms. Examples include thyroid medication, inhalers for asthma or other breathing issues, medicines for attention deficit or hyperactivity disorder, steroids, decongestants, and some anti-depressants.

Some medications can cause anxiety symptoms when you stop taking them, reduce the dosage, or miss a dose. For example, anti-anxiety medicines like Xanax (alprazolam), Klonopin (clonazepam), Valium (diazepam), and other benzodiazepine medicines or heart medications like betablockers.

If you think a prescription medicine is contributing to your anxiety, talk to your healthcare provider or pharmacist. **Do not change** the amount of

Form 3-02: Chemical Triggers Checklist

Mark any chemical triggers that apply to you:

☐ Caffeine or other stimulants

☐ Alcohol

☐ Smoking

☐ Marijuana

☐ Street drugs

☐ Over-the-counter drugs or supplements

☐ Prescription medications

☐ Hormone changes from menstrual periods, menopause, etc.

any prescription medicine you take without checking with your healthcare provider.

Female Hormone Changes

Changing hormone levels can make a woman more anxious or depressed. Birth control pills or other medications can affect hormone levels. Levels also change during the menstrual cycle, during and after pregnancy, during infertility treatment, following a hysterectomy, and around menopause. Hormone replacement medications or other medicines can affect hormone levels.

Talk to your healthcare provider or pharmacist if you think hormones or related medications contribute to your anxiety symptoms.

Story: Liah

Liah realized Chemical Triggers contributed to her anxiety. To keep up with her busy schedule, she was drinking four large cups of coffee each morning and at least one energy drink every afternoon. She also realized that she tended to feel more stressed and anxious during the week before her menstrual period.

She gradually reduced the amount of coffee she had in the morning, stopped drinking energy drinks in the afternoon, and started paying attention to where she was in her menstrual cycle.

Do **You** have Chemical Triggers?

Mark your possible triggers on Form 3-02: Chemical Triggers Checklist (page 47). If you think these chemicals are contributing to your anxiety, consider reducing or eliminating them – following the cautions above.

External Stress Triggers

Stress can be a big trigger for anxiety or panic. External stress can include school stress, work stress, stress from not working, loneliness, interpersonal stress, bullying, relationship or family stress, conflict with other people (boss, coworkers, neighbors, friends, family members, parents, children, etc.), body image issues, gender identity issues, sexuality issues, stress from a difficult commute, money worries, worry about family members and friends, physical illness or chronic conditions, pain, uncertainty about the future, stress about the economy, and so on. Think about all possible sources of stress in your life.

Story: Raj

Raj quickly realized that he had several external stress triggers. His long commute to and from work each day was really draining. Plus, he was working long hours and trying to balance the demands of a stressful job with the needs of his extended family.

Story: Liah

One major external stress trigger for Liah was her job at a high-powered marketing firm. Her bosses expected her to work overtime without additional pay. As a result, she and her boyfriend were arguing about how much time she spent at work, and she did not have time for relaxation or exercise, which had been her stress relievers during college.

Form 3-03: External Stress List

Job:

_____

Commute:

_____

Home/family/personal relationships:

_____

Certain people:

_____

Medical conditions:

_____

Money/economy/financial uncertainty:

_____

Other:

_____

_____

_____

_____

_____

_____

Story: Amanda

At first, Amanda had trouble identifying her external stress triggers because she had become so used to them. The divorce, financial stress and uncertainty, and being a newly single parent to young children were easy to identify as stresses.

It was harder for Amanda to identify that her mother contributed to her anxiety. Amanda's mom has been very critical of her all Amanda's life. As Amanda thought about external stresses, she realized that having to move back in with her parents was a big stressor because she knew her mother would see the divorce as a failure on Amanda's part.

Do **You** have External Stress Triggers?

List all the external stresses in your life on Form 3-03: External Stress List (page 49). Include all the stress triggers you can think of, even if you have been coping with them for years. Make a complete, accurate list even if you feel you are not "stressed" by them.

The more stresses on your list, the more likely that external stress triggers play a role in your anxiety and panic. In Chapter 9: Reducing Your Triggers, you will use this information to begin reducing these triggers.

Self-Talk and Unrealistic Self-Demands Triggers

Everything that happens in your life—events, demands, other people's actions, future plans, and external stress—gets filtered through what you say to yourself, how you think about events, how you think about yourself, what you expect of yourself, and what you expect from other people.

Negative self-talk and unrealistic self-demands contribute to anxiety and panic by making external stress worse. Supportive self-talk and realistic self-demands reduce the impact of external stresses and help protect you from anxiety.

Listen to what you say out loud <u>and</u> to what you think silently to yourself. How you talk to yourself, and what you expect, can make external stress more—or less—stressful.

Form 3-04: Negative Self-Talk Checklist

Do you:

☐ Criticize yourself?

☐ Call yourself hurtful names?

☐ Point out your shortcomings or focus on the negative about yourself?

☐ See yourself as helpless, incompetent, or weak?

☐ Feel vulnerable?

☐ Feel unable to protect yourself, take care of yourself, or cope?

☐ Focus on problems, rather than solutions or coping?

☐ Focus on the negative about your past, other people, or the world?

☐ Think about what can go wrong and expect the worst?

Negative Self-Talk

Any kind of negative self-talk makes panic and worry more likely. Three common types of negative self-talk are self-criticism, viewing yourself as helpless, and expecting the worst or focusing on the negatives in your life.

Other examples of negative self-talk include thinking about things in black-or-white terms ("perfect" or "disaster"), name-calling ("stupid", "weak"), assuming problems are permanent ("always", "never"), and blaming yourself without looking at all the factors involved ("all my fault").

Check each item on Form 3-04: Negative Self-Talk Checklist (page 51) that may apply to you.

Unrealistic Self-Demands

Many people who have anxiety or panic don't realize they are making unrealistic demands of themselves. Perhaps you are the person everyone tends to turn to for help. Maybe you don't want to let anyone down, disappoint anyone, or have anyone be upset with you. You may want to make everyone

Form 3-05: Unrealistic Self-Demands Checklist

Do you tend to:

☐ Feel responsible for things that are out of your control?

☐ Take responsibility for everyone and everything?

☐ Feel guilty if things go wrong?

☐ Feel responsible for everyone's happiness or safety? Are you the person everyone turns to for help? Do you try to fix everyone?

☐ Expect perfection – even if you don't think of it in those words? Do others say you are a perfectionist?

☐ Have expectations so high that you constantly worry about failing?

☐ Never want to let anyone down?

☐ Want to never make a mistake, or look weak, or upset anyone?

☐ Feel the need to please everyone or have everybody's agreement?

☐ Avoid disagreeing or stating an opinion? Are you afraid to say what you want or how you feel?

☐ Expect that you should never feel anxious?

☐ See anxiety as a failure on your part?

☐ Feel you should always be in control?

☐ Think you should never need anyone or need help?

☐ Demand certainty? Want guaranteed safety?

☐ Become very upset about the fact that life is unfair at times? Do you demand that the world and other people be fair?

happy and fix every problem. You want to do everything perfectly and never make a mistake or look foolish. You do not want to appear weak or anxious. You want to behave perfectly.

It is important to strive to live up to your ideals, but it is unrealistic to expect or demand that you achieve your ideals perfectly in every way and every day. It is unrealistic to believe that you will never make mistakes. It is unrealistic to feel you must fix everyone's problems, or to demand that the world be fair.

You cannot be perfect. You do not control other people's decisions and actions. Telling yourself that you "have to" do something that is not under your control creates more stress as your mind argues with itself: "I have to" "But I can't." But I have to." But I can't!" But **I have to!**" "But **I can't!!**"

Think about what you ask of yourself as you complete Form 3-05: Unrealistic Self-Demands Checklist.

Do **You** have Self-Talk Triggers?

Review the items you checked off on the forms above. Which self-talk triggers do you have? Notice when you talk to yourself, or think about yourself, in ways that may trigger anxiety. Liah and Carlos found their self-talk and self-demands contributed to their panic attacks.

Story: Liah

Liah admits that she is a perfectionist and wanted to show her new boss that she's a hard worker. She can be hard on herself and has high expectations for success. When she makes even a small mistake, she tells herself, "That was so stupid! How could I mess up like that? What is wrong with me?" She says things like, "If I don't get things right, I will be fired, and I will never find another good job."

Story: Carlos

Carlos has always taken pride in helping and supporting his large family. "I am the rock". Everyone comes to him for help and advice, but he never lets himself turn to anyone else for help or support. He tells himself his family would think he was "weak and unreliable" if he asked anyone for help. "I am the man of the family. I am responsible for them." He does not realize that while his family appreciates his help, they feel shut out when he spurns their offers of help.

Past Event Triggers

You remember the past. Past events, and the lessons learned from them, affect you in the present.

Your brain not only learns from what happens to you; it also learns from what happens to other people. It learns lessons from what friends and family tell you, what you hear on the radio, what you see in social media, videos, TV, or movies, and what you read online or in newspapers, magazines, and books.

Some of these lessons are helpful and still apply, like not touching a hot stove or looking both ways before crossing the street. Other lessons are not helpful or not true, like believing panic attacks are dangerous (you will learn how panic attacks are uncomfortable but NOT dangerous below) or believing that because you were helpless or treated badly as a child that you continue to be helpless as an adult and that bad things will always happen to you.

Lessons your brain learns from past experiences may be true *or false*. They may be helpful or *unhelpful*. They may *or may not* apply to you currently.

Read on to explore how, and why, unhelpful lessons from past events can trigger anxiety or panic.

How Past Events Can Trigger Anxiety

Past events affect when and where you panic

For example, if you had a panic attack while driving a car, you will be more likely to panic in the future while driving. Because you had a panic attack while driving, your Reacting Brain may now associate driving with panicking. If you had a panic attack while on an airplane, you would be more likely to panic when flying. If you had one while swimming, you would tend to panic when swimming. And so on.

Childhood Events

Were your parents ever separated or divorced? Did a parent die, leave, or have a serious illness? Have you lived with a stepparent or foster parent?

Did you ever run away from home for more than one day?

Have you ever tried to harm or kill yourself?

Did a parent or other adult in your household:

- Frequently swear at you, insult you, or put you down?

- Act in a way that made you afraid that you would be physically hurt?

- Push, grab, shove, or slap you? Hit you so hard that you had marks or were injured?

When you were a child, did an adult or person 5 or more years older than you ever:

- Touch or fondle you in a sexual way, or have you touch them in a sexual way?

- Attempt or have oral, anal, or vaginal intercourse with you?

Did you live with anyone who:

- Was a problem drinker, an alcoholic, or a drug abuser?

- Was mentally ill, depressed, or attempted suicide?

- Committed a serious crime or went to prison?

Were any of your parents:

- Yelled at or verbally abused at home?

- Involved in a physical fight, attacked, threatened or beaten?

Story: Raj

Raj's Past Event was becoming physically sick after eating in a social situation. His Reacting Brain learned the following unhelpful lessons: "I might get sick and throw up if I eat in public. This would be unbearably embarrassing. The best solution is to avoid all eating in public and to leave if I feel any odd sensations in my stomach."

Past events can determine your fears

Past events also affect **what fears** come to your mind when you panic and what your brain thinks is dangerous. For example, if you or someone close to you had a serious illness, when you panic you are more likely to fear that something is medically wrong. On the other hand, if you had heard or read about someone going crazy, you would worry about your *mental* health, not your physical health.

Story: Carlos

When Carlos had panic symptoms, he feared he was having a heart attack or stroke. He thought, "I have physical symptoms. I must have a physical problem." His fear of a heart attack was especially strong because his father and grandfather both died from heart attacks. He vividly recalled seeing his grandfather and his father die and he was convinced that "I am just like them." He never thought about the fact that his father and grandfather had both been overweight, never exercised, had high blood pressure and diabetes, and did not follow their doctors' advice.

Carlos' past events were seeing his father and grandfather die of heart attacks. His unhelpful lessons were "I am just like them. I will die of a heart attack. Physical symptoms are the sign of a serious physical disease."

Lessons can be unhelpful or untrue

Your brain can learn **unhelpful lessons from past events** that cause it to keep sending messages of danger. For example, if bad things happened to you at a time when you were helpless or vulnerable, your brain remembers, and may continue to react as if you are *still* helpless and vulnerable. It may have learned lessons like the world is a dangerous place, bad things are likely

---

Traumatic Stress

Very bad experiences that create feelings of horror can be particularly difficult to deal with and can cause ongoing stress responses known as post-traumatic stress disorder (PTSD). We are talking here about extreme events such as being robbed at gunpoint, believing your life or the life of a loved one is in danger, being in a life-threatening situation, being raped, assaulted or molested, seeing someone die or being in combat, and feeling helpless and horrified.

After events like these, you may feel emotionally numb, you may be unable to remember parts of what happened, or you may feel cut off from others or from your future. You may have intense responses as if you are reliving what happened. You may have nightmares, trouble sleeping and concentrating, be easily startled, or always feel on guard.

If you think you may have PTSD, see a licensed mental health therapist who is knowledgeable in its treatment. Panic attacks can be part of PTSD and the skills in this book may be helpful. However, PTSD treatment involves more than what is covered in this book.

---

and can happen at any time, other people are unreliable or untrustworthy, and so on.

Things we experience as children can affect our thinking and actions years later. Review the list of Childhood Events (page 55) and see if you had similar experiences. If you did, consider how these events might influence how you think and act today. When you fill out Form 3-06: Past Events List (page 59), include any important events and the lessons you may have learned.

These lessons may have been true or helpful at some time in the past. However, your brain may continue to react as if they are true now—even after things have changed and you are *not* in fact helpless or in danger.

Story: Amanda

What Amanda remembers clearly about her childhood is "My father drank, and I never knew what to expect. I would hear my parents fighting in the middle of the night. One time he was driving drunk and he crashed the car while I was asleep in the backseat. I woke up in a panic. Ever since, I've felt panicky riding in the backseat of a car. Lately I've been getting anxious when I start to go to sleep, or when I'm in a car, even if I'm driving. I worry that if I have a panic attack while driving, I'll crash the car."

Amanda's past events include growing up with an alcohol-abusing father and waking up to a car crash. Her unhelpful lessons include that it can be dangerous to ride in a car or to fall asleep. Her Reacting Brain may have also learned unhelpful lessons such as she cannot trust other people, that she is vulnerable, and that cars are likely to crash.

Story: Liah

When Liah was ten, her mom was hospitalized because of a serious depression. Liah was scared and alone. She was told that her mother had had "a nervous breakdown." Liah worried that her mother's condition was her fault for being bad, so she decided to try and "always be a good girl." Since then, she has tried to please everyone. She feels responsible for making her mother happy and feels guilty when she resents this responsibility. When she panics, she is scared of "going crazy" or fears "having a breakdown like my mother."

Liah's past events include her mother's depression. Liah learned several unhelpful lessons. She learned (wrongly) that she caused her mother to become depressed and leave her, that she is responsible for her mother's happiness, that she must please everyone, make everyone happy, and be perfect or else something bad will happen, and that she is likely to "go crazy" or "have a nervous breakdown" like her mother.

Do **You** have Anxiety Triggered by Past Events?

Think about *when* you panic and your *fears about panic*. Look for connections to things that happened in the past to you or to other people.

Write down the past events and unhelpful lessons that your brain may have learned on Form 3-06: Past Events List .

Form 3-06: Past Events List

List past events and any unhelpful lessons your brain may have learned from each event.

Event:

_____

Unhelpful Lesson(s):

_____

Event:

_____

Unhelpful Lesson(s):

_____

Event:

_____

Unhelpful Lesson(s):

_____

Event:

_____

Unhelpful Lesson(s):

_____

Event:

_____

Unhelpful Lesson(s):

_____

Event:

_____

Unhelpful Lesson(s):

_____

Your Triggers and the Panic/Anxiety Cycle

Your triggers, your brain, your body, your thoughts, and your actions all interact with one another. They can either weaken the cycle of anxiety and panic—or strengthen it.

Some anxiety is an inescapable part of life. Anyone will panic if enough triggers are activated. Sometimes one trigger is enough to cause panic attacks; sometimes several triggers must be hit.

The bottom line is, if your triggers are hit hard enough you're going to panic. This is how your brain works. Unfortunately, the ways people naturally think and act when afraid make anxiety and panic worse in the long run, creating a vicious cycle.

The Good News

This book teaches you how to break this vicious cycle. Chapter 2: The Anxiety Cycle explains the anxiety cycle from start to finish. This Section helps you understand your personal cycle of anxiety and panic which prepares you to learn how to change it.

My explanations should match your experiences and make sense of them. You will understand why certain natural responses do not work and be ready to learn what *will work*.

Triggers Send Messages of Threat

Review your personal triggers briefly, remembering that one trigger can affect others:

- Genetic factors and relatives with anxiety on Form 3-01: Relatives with Anxiety (page 45)

- Chemical triggers on Form 3-02: Chemical Triggers Checklist (page 47)

- External stresses on Form 3-03: External Stress List (page 49)

- Negative self-talk on Form 3-04: Negative Self-Talk Checklist (page 51)

- Unrealistic self-demands on Form 3-05: Unrealistic Self-Demands Checklist (page 52)

- Past events and unhelpful lessons on Form 3-06: Past Events List (page 59).

Genetic or Chemical Triggers Make You More Likely to Panic

Genetically, you may have inherited a tendency toward panic. You may have a more responsive "sports-car-type" nervous system, compared to other people's slower-to-react "minivan-type" nervous system.

Chemicals prime you for panic by revving you up, physically or emotionally, or by creating panic sensations.

Triggers Interact to Send Messages of Threat and Danger

External stresses send the message "Threat! You have all these stresses!" External stress can make you feel tired, overwhelmed, or pressured. Stresses of any kind increase the likelihood of panic, especially if you lack good stress management skills.

Negative self-talk can send messages like "Threat! You are vulnerable, weak, or incompetent. You are a loser. Panic is horrible and intolerable! Nothing will work out. This program won't work."

Unrealistic self-demands send the message, "Threat! You will not live up to your unrealistic ideals or self-demands. You won't handle stresses like you think you should. You need to be perfect, and you won't be. You must never be anxious or make a mistake. You must please, or fix, everyone."

Unhelpful lessons from past events send messages like "Threat! You will mess up like you did before. You are vulnerable or helpless like you were before. The world is dangerous. Other people cannot be trusted! If something bad *might* happen, it *will* happen. Whatever bad thing happened before will happen again. Bad things that happened to others will happen to you."

Messages of Threat Go to your Reacting Brain

Messages of threat or danger go directly to your caveman Reacting Brain, whose job is to respond to threats and protect you. The good news is this part of the brain reacts instantly when you are physically threatened, and fast reactions can save your life. That is its job. It is devoted to your safety and protection.

The bad news is that this part of the brain is really dumb. It reacts to *any* message of threat—even when you are not in physical danger—which means when your triggers send messages of threat, your primitive brain may needlessly activate the panic response. In other words, it is devoted but dumb! It can be well-intentioned but misinformed.

Reducing Triggers

I will explain how to reduce your triggers in the next section (see Chapter 9 Reduce Your Triggers). If you see any changes you can make now that will help reduce your triggers, feel free to start making those changes.

Chapter Summary

Completing this chapter has helped you identify your anxiety triggers. Triggers are an important factor in causing or increasing anxiety and panic. Many triggers can be eliminated or changed, as we will discuss later.

Track your progress using Form 3-99: Completed Chapter 3. Note things you have learned, or been surprised by, in this chapter.

Form 3-99: Completed Chapter 3

Date completed: _____

Lessons learned: _____

_____

Chapter **4:**

Puzzling Panic Patterns

"I understood why I panicked when I was pushing to meet a deadline, but it made no sense why I'd panic on vacation or while relaxing watching TV." — David

"The worst was when I would wake up in a panic in the middle of the night. — Linda"

"I don't why I'm having panic now! I've handled stresses for years." — Barbara

Sometimes you can quickly identify your anxiety trigger(s). You can predict when you are likely to panic. Other times, panic seems puzzling and hard to understand.

People frequently ask why panic can come out of the blue for no apparent reason. For example, some people have anxiety or panic attacks when they are relaxing or sleeping. It can be puzzling to panic when you are not feeling stressed or not consciously thinking about danger. People also wonder how panic and worry are different, and how they can interact. This chapter answers these questions.

Why Panic While Relaxing?

You may panic when relaxing because your Reacting Brain is acting on an unhelpful lesson it learned in the past. It may believe that you are vulnerable or that the world is dangerous, therefore it thinks relaxing is dangerous because you let down your guard and become vulnerable to attack.

Overcoming Anxiety and Panic interactive guide

63

Anxiety or panic symptoms may occur for some people when they begin learning and practicing relaxation techniques. Relaxation may feel like loss of control, or relaxation-induced changes in physical sensations may be misinterpreted as dangerous.

If you have been chronically hyperventilating or overbreathing, the change in oxygen/carbon dioxide balance when you relax and slow down your breathing, can make you feel like you are not getting enough air. Until you learn that this uncomfortable feeling is temporary and harmless, it can scare you and cause your Reacting Brain to jump into (unnecessary) action to "protect" you. For more information, see Short of Breath (page 76). Breaking the cycle of chronic hyperventilation by practicing belly breathing and relaxing will remove this trigger.

Why Panic During Sleep?

You may be asleep, but *your caveman bodyguard, the Reacting Brain, never sleeps*. It is always looking for signs of possible danger. Your Reacting Brain may react to a noise or sound that it associates with threat. It may react to a dream because it cannot tell the difference between dreams and reality.

If the bodily sensations of anxiety or panic scare you, your Reacting Brain will have noticed your fear and may have decided that these bodily changes must be a threat (otherwise you would not be frightened of them). Since everyone's body has thousands of tiny physical changes happening automatically all the time, whether awake or asleep, the Reacting Brain may jump in to "save you" from normal, automatic, unconscious bodily changes, so you wake in a panic.

Panic attacks during sleep may be triggered by changes in breathing caused by chronically hyperventilating as described above. Other breathing changes during sleep that may trigger panic include snoring or interrupted breathing due to sleep apnea or other physical issues.

If you feel chronically tired even after a full night's sleep, if your bed partner comments that you snore loudly or stop breathing, or if you frequently wake up gasping for air, check with your healthcare provider to see if you might have sleep apnea or other medical issues. Treating such problems can help improve anxiety and overall health.

Story: Liah

Liah sought anxiety treatment, in part, because she had begun waking up suddenly in the middle of the night in a panic. Her heart was racing. Her body was sweaty, but she was shivering and cold. She felt like she couldn't take a deep breath and, even scarier for her, she felt like she was not connected to her body. Liah feared she was having a "nervous breakdown" like her mother.

Why Panic When You Do Not Feel Stressed?

You may panic because triggers other than external stress are activating your anxiety response. You may panic for the same reasons people panic during sleep or relaxation (as explained above).

Why Panic When You Are Not Thinking About Danger?

When you use your Thinking Brain to think, you know *that* you are thinking and *what* you are thinking. Your Thinking Brain is conscious and verbal; it works with words and logic. This is an oversimplification of our complex brain but accurate enough for overcoming panic.

Your primitive, protective caveman Reacting Brain, on the other hand, reacts automatically without consulting you or getting permission. Its responses to danger are automatic and unthinking. It is *not conscious*. It is *not verbal*. It is *not logical*.

When your Reacting Brain thinks that you are threatened, *or when it sees that you are afraid*, it remembers everything about that moment and associates it with danger to you. It can decide that the situation, the people around you, your thoughts, your sensations—anything and everything—are signs of danger. As a result, more and more things can trigger it to react.

Why Panic Now If You Have Been Stressed for Years?

You may be panicking now because you are more stressed than you realize. This is especially likely if your stresses have been increasing gradually over time.

The myth of the "boiled frog" explains how this happens. The legend is that if you put a frog in a pan of boiling water, it will immediately jump out. But if you put the frog in a pan of cool water and gradually increase the heat, the frog will sit there until it is boiled. (No frogs were harmed in the telling of this story.)

Are you a "boiled frog?" Have you been ignoring stresses as they were building up? Do you take on more and more stress because each little increase doesn't seem like much at the time?

It's like standing in water that starts out around your ankles ("That's not bad."), moves to your hips ("Okay, there's more, but I'm okay."), rises to your chest ("All right, I can handle this."), until the next thing you know the water is over your head and you're drowning.

If you make impossible demands of yourself—like never saying no, not wanting to let anyone down ever, wanting to take care of everything for everyone—panic may be a signal that you need to change. Negative self-talk or impossible self-demands may be routine and familiar but still contribute to stress, anxiety and panic.

How Do Panic and Worry Differ? How Do They Interact?

Two key differences between panic and worry are duration and intensity. The panic response is more intense, but temporary. Worry is less intense but can continue for years. See page 68 and page 69.

Remember, panic is the normal fight-or-flight response to danger; it is just going off when it is not needed. When faced with real danger, you immediately go from relaxation to fight-or-flight. This fast, automatic response saves your life. After reaching safety, your body returns to its previous relaxed state.

Think of nature films you may have seen. The gazelles are grazing peacefully in the grass. A lion attacks! The gazelles instantly flee, leaping to safety in a

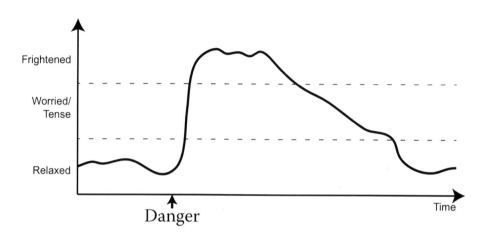

Figure 4-01: Normal Fight-or-Flight Response

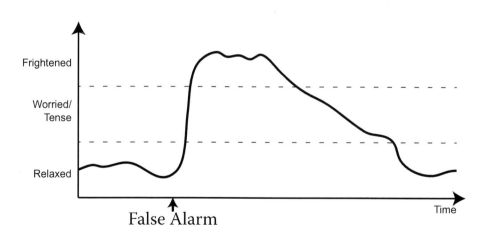

Figure 4-02: False Alarm Fight-or-Flight Response

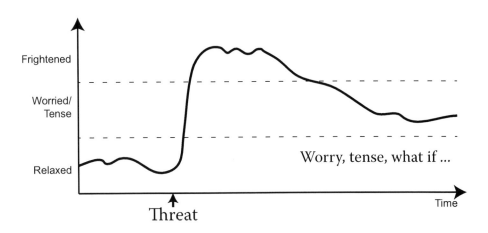

Figure 4-03: Panic Leading to Worry

panic. Then when the danger is past, they resume peacefully grazing. This is how the fight-or-flight response is supposed to work.

As you now know, when the flight-or-flight response goes off in the absence of danger, this misfiring in response to a false alarm is called a panic attack.

Just like the gazelles, you start out in a normal state of relaxation. Then something triggers your Reacting Brain to send *a false alarm* of "danger." Adrenaline is released, readying you to run or fight. After the adrenaline subsides—if you understand that the reaction is temporary and harmless— you return to your normal relaxed state. The experience is unpleasant, but temporary. No big deal.

But what if you do not understand that the panic is unpleasant, but harmless? You might not relax. You might stay worried, tense, and anxious. Worry is not temporary. It is physically milder than a panic attack, but lasts far longer and can become a chronic, ongoing problem. Panic can lead to worry, and worry– because it keeps you tense and on guard– can lead to more panic.

Here are two common ways that panic and worry interact.

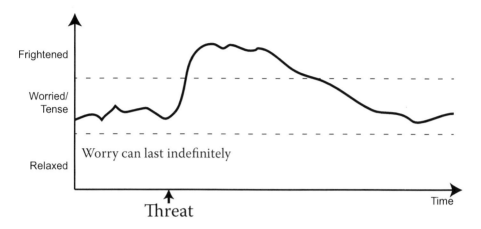

Figure 4-04: Worry Leading to More Worry

From Relaxed to Panic to Worried

You are relaxed. Something triggers a misfiring of panic, BUT you do not understand what is happening so after the panic subsides, instead of relaxing again, you worry about that attack and/or you worry about having another panic attack. You think, "What was that? Will it happen again? What if it gets worse? What if I can't control it and something awful happens? What if ….? What if ….?" You stay worried and tense, on "partial red alert." This makes additional panic attacks even more likely because by feeling tense, worried, and hyper-alert for danger you are already halfway there.

From Worried to Panic to More Worried

Perhaps you *do not* start out relaxed. Perhaps you are living with ongoing stress, worry, tension, and/or unrealistic self-demands. As you have learned, these can trigger a panic attack. Then, after having had a panic attack, you add even more worry to your original worries because you now worry about panic attacks in addition to everything else you worried about before. More worry creates more panics—which create more worries—which create more panics, and off you go!

Panic is more intense than worry, but it only lasts for a short time. Your body is *designed* to have short bursts of fight-or-flight arousal; it is *not* designed to stay chronically tense or worried over long periods of time. Later in this book you will learn several techniques that can help you deal with fears, stress, and worry.

Chronic negative emotions can be bad for you. These include chronic worry, chronic anger, chronic depression, chronic cynicism, chronic hostility, or chronic stress. If you have any of these conditions, consider getting professional help to reduce your chronic negative emotions, in addition to treating your fear of panic. See the Appendix for information on finding a therapist.

Chapter Summary

In this chapter you learned more about panic attacks that otherwise seem hard to understand because they happen in the absence of common triggers. You have also learned about the differences between panic and worry, and how one can feed the other.

Track your progress using Form 4-99: Completed Chapter 4. Note things you have learned, or been surprised by, in this chapter.

Form 4-99: Completed Chapter 4

Date completed: _____

Lessons learned:

_____

Chapter 5

Your Anxiety or Panic Sensations

"Understanding what was causing the feelings in my body made all the difference." – William

"No one had ever explained what was happening in a way that made sense to me. Thank you!" — Jennifer

Anxiety is very physical. It can cause many different sensations. You can easily be frightened by these sensations and–if you do not understand what is happening–you can mistakenly focus your energy on fighting or running from panic, instead of finding and fixing the real problem: what triggered panic to misfire in the first place.

In this chapter, I explain the causes of anxiety or panic sensations, why they are harmless, and the original protective purpose for each sensation.

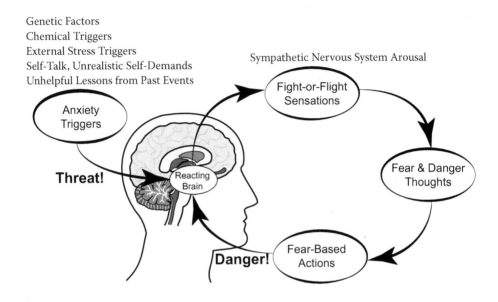

Genetic Factors
Chemical Triggers
External Stress Triggers
Self-Talk, Unrealistic Self-Demands
Unhelpful Lessons from Past Events

Figure 5-01: Anxiety Leading to Fight-or-Flight Sensations

What sensations do *you* get in response to anxiety? On Form 5-01: Anxiety or Panic Sensations rate each sensation you have experienced while you were anxious or panicky. How much were you bothered by each sensation?

There are no right or wrong answers. People who experience all of these sensations have gotten better.

Rate each sensation you have experienced using this 0-3 scale:

0 None, did not happen or did not bother me

1 Mild, bothered me a little but not much

2 Moderate, bothered me and was unpleasant at times

3 Severe, this sensation bothered me a lot

Form 5-01: Anxiety or Panic Sensations

Sensation	Rating 0-3
Fast heartbeat, racing or pounding heart	
Chest tightness or chest pain	
Muscle tension	
Scared, nervous, afraid	
Fear of dying	
Fear of worst happening	
Feeling shaky, trembling, or weak	
Feeling unsteady	
Fear of losing control	
Short of breath, like you can't breathe, or not getting enough air	
Feeling hot or flushed	
Sweaty or clammy	
Tingling, numbness, or feeling cold	
Dizzy, unsteady, light-headed, or faint	
Visual changes like blurriness, spots, dark, light, tunnel vision, etc.	
Feeling unreal or like you are not present	
Nausea, queasiness, butterflies, knots in your stomach, other abdominal symptoms	
Feeling of choking, lump in the throat, can't swallow	
Feeling like you cannot think or concentrate	

Other physical sensations:

_____

_____

What Happens and Why?

For each symptom on your Anxiety or Panic Sensations list you will learn what cases each sensation and its *lifesaving, helpful, protective purpose.* Focus on the information that is most relevant and helpful to you. You can skip any sensations you have not experienced.

Read this information slowly, so you can really think about it and take it in. Read it as many times as you need to understand what happens in your body when you feel anxious or panicky. If you have a sensation that is not covered here, ask your healthcare provider or therapist.

Fast Heartbeat, Racing or Pounding Heart

Your heart may beat faster, beat harder, or feel like it is pounding. Another word for this is palpitations.

These changes occur because your Reacting Brain signals your heart to start pumping more blood to your muscles quickly. The reason for this is that blood carries oxygen and glucose to fuel your fighting muscles. Since the Reacting Brain thinks you may have to run or fight, it wants to make sure the muscles have all the fuel they need.

Chest Tightness or Chest Pain

The Reacting Brain tenses your muscles because it thinks you will have to run or fight at any second and it wants you to be prepared. Muscle tension in the chest can naturally cause feelings of pressure, tightness, or pain. Chest breathing and hyperventilating (see page 76) can increase these feelings.

Muscle Tension

The Reacting Brain signals your muscles to tense up and get ready for action. After all, you don't prepare for a fight by relaxing! This is why you may notice muscle tension, shaking, or trembling.

Muscle tension can cause headaches, other head sensations, or pain in your neck, back, shoulders, and elsewhere. Your Reacting Brain tenses the muscles in your back to help protect you in case you get ambushed from behind.

Sidebar: Stress Reactions

Complex biochemical, anatomical, and physiological systems are involved in the fight-or-flight response to threats and stress. If you are interested in more detail, an excellent starting point is **Why Zebras Don't Get Ulcers** by Robert M. Sapolsky (Henry Holt and Company, 2004).

The Reacting Brain also instinctively tightens the muscles of your stomach, your soft underbelly, where you are physically vulnerable to attack. Tensed stomach muscles can contribute to feeling short of breath, as you will read below.

You may notice muscle pain from tensing, or jaw pain from clenching your jaw or grinding your teeth. Tensed muscles can make you look bigger. And fiercely baring your gritted teeth may convince an enemy to back away. Think of a dog growling and baring its teeth at anything it thinks is a threat.

Shaky or Trembling

Shaking or trembling can be visible or just felt inside your body. The Reacting Brain tenses your muscles, and adrenaline revs up your body to run or fight—but you are *not* running or fighting. This is like putting a car in neutral and pressing the gas pedal, the engine races and the car shakes but does not move. This muscle tension exercise will help you understand shaking.

Muscle Tension Exercise

Hold your arm straight out in front of you and tense all the muscles in your hand and arm. (Don't cause yourself pain.) Tense, tense; harder, harder. Tense more, and even more, and hold the tension.

Notice how your hand and arm start to tremble and shake. The more you tense, the more they shake. The harder you try to stop the shaking by tensing, the worse you make it.

This not only demonstrates how muscle tension creates trembling, it is also an example of how fighting anxiety does not work. Just as you cannot steady your hand by desperately tensing it, you cannot lessen panic by desperately fighting it.

Weakness or "Jelly Legs"

Feelings of weakness, wobbly "jelly legs," or inner trembling can be both a result of muscle tension and a response to the surge of adrenaline getting you revved up to run or fight. Since you are **not** running or fighting, the adrenaline is not being used. As a result, it can take a while for your body to calm down.

Short of Breath or Not Getting Enough Air

Feeling as if you cannot breathe, or as if you are not getting enough air, is common with anxiety and panic. There are two reasons for this feeling: tensed muscles and hyperventilating.

Tensed Muscles

In addition to tensing your fighting muscles, the Reacting Brain tenses your abdominal muscles. As mentioned above, your Reacting Brain is trying to protect your soft underbelly where you are vulnerable to attack.

Do this quick exercise. It will help you understand the effect of tense muscles on feeling short of breath.

Tensed Muscles Breathing Exercise

Tense all the muscles in your trunk (chest and abdomen), tight, tight, tight (but without causing pain). Now, try to breathe while you keep them tensed.

Right! It's hard to breathe when your muscles are tense. Even tensing just your belly muscles (lower abdomen) can make you feel like you cannot get a deep breath or are not getting enough air. This is one reason that learning and practicing belly breathing can help, see page 147.

Hyperventilating and Oxygen/Carbon Dioxide Balance

Breathing in excess of your body's current needs is called hyperventilating or overbreathing and can make you feel anxious or short of breath by altering the balance of oxygen and carbon dioxide in your blood. You may hyperventilate briefly when you feel threatened or tense. Sometimes this becomes a habit and people hyperventilate much of the time (chronically).

Carbon dioxide levels that are unusually low or high can trigger feelings of anxiety and panic. Hyperventilating can cause the carbon dioxide level in your blood to drop, making you feel short of breath and anxious–*even though you are getting enough air and oxygen*. Changes in the carbon dioxide level can happen quickly—based on a single big breath—and once started may take some time to return to normal.

Breathing brings air into the lungs. Blood vessels in the lungs absorb oxygen from the air and carry it to the muscles. Muscle activity uses oxygen and glucose for energy, creating carbon dioxide as a byproduct. Carbon dioxide goes into the blood, which carries it back to the lungs to be breathed out.

Normally the oxygen coming in from the lungs, oxygen used by the muscles, carbon dioxide produced by muscles, and carbon dioxide removed by breathing are balanced:

- When you relax: you breathe more slowly, bringing in less oxygen. Your muscles use less oxygen, putting out less carbon dioxide. The levels of oxygen and carbon dioxide remain balanced.

- When you exercise, run, or fight: you breathe harder and faster, bringing in more oxygen; your muscles work harder, using up more oxygen and putting out more carbon dioxide. The levels of oxygen coming in and the levels of carbon dioxide going out are balanced.

During an anxiety attack, your Reacting Brain automatically speeds up your breathing because it thinks your muscles will need a lot of oxygen for fighting or fleeing. Your muscles, on the other hand, say "I don't know what *you* think is going on. I'm just sitting here trying to relax (or sleep, or drive the car, or whatever)."

Since your muscles are not converting oxygen into carbon dioxide, your blood oxygen level remains high while your carbon dioxide level declines. This can cause a perceptible, *but harmless*, decrease in blood flow to the head, hands, and feet resulting in feelings of lightheadedness, tingling, numbness, cold hands, paler skin, and twitching or cramping.

Your body is getting *more air* than it needs, but paradoxically, you feel like you are getting *less air* than you need. The natural reaction to feeling you are not getting enough air or to feeling short of breath is to take bigger chest breaths and breathe in more oxygen, which increases the imbalance between oxygen and carbon dioxide, making you feel even worse! Sometimes just one particularly deep or fast breath can make you feel like you are not getting enough air.

Hyperventilation can happen without gasping for air. You can chronically overbreathe without realizing it. People who chronically hyperventilate often feel out of breath. If you have become used to continually hyperventilating, you may react to either exercise or relaxation with anxiety, chest tightness, fatigue, or muscle pain.

Note: Hyperventilation can also be caused by medical conditions that are not related to anxiety. If you find you are hyperventilating in situations that are not anxiety provoking, ask your healthcare provider about other possible causes.

You Don't Need to Breathe into a Bag

If you feel short of breath when you are anxious or panicky, you may have been told to breathe into a paper bag. The idea was that by breathing into a bag, you would breathe in the same air repeatedly. Each time you re-breathe the air, your muscles use up some oxygen in the bag, replacing it with carbon dioxide, bringing the levels of oxygen and carbon dioxide back into balance.

You do not need a paper bag. You accomplish the same goal safely and effectively with low and slow, rhythmic belly breathing, using your diaphragm. See the instructions on page 147. If you want to learn this skill now, feel free to skip ahead and return here when you are done.

Oxygen and carbon dioxide levels can also be rebalanced by brief exercise or by holding your breath. I generally recommend belly breathing because, unlike exercise, you can do belly breathing anywhere, at any time. Also, belly breathing has other benefits including helping muscles relax, while holding your breath can increase muscle tension.

Feeling Hot

The Reacting Brain sends lots of blood to the big muscles to bring them oxygen and fuel for running or fighting. To do this, it expands blood vessels to some areas of the body. This can make you feel hot or flushed.

Sweaty or Clammy

Sweating cools you and prevents overheating. The Reacting Brain does not want you to overheat while running or fighting for your life, so it makes you sweat. Plus, if you are slippery and some enemy grabs you, you may be able to slip away and survive.

Tingling, Numbness, or Feeling Cold

Feelings of cold, tingling, or numbness can be caused by hyperventilating and related changes in blood flow. If, as a result of hyperventilating, blood oxygen levels are high and carbon dioxide levels are low, blood vessels contract, causing tingling and numbness.

Even if you are not hyperventilating, the Reacting Brain pulls blood away from your extremities (hands, feet, and head) for two protective reasons:

- First, it is redirecting blood to the main fighting muscles because it wants those muscles to have lots of fuel, so you can fight at maximum capacity. It pulls blood away from the extremities and sends it to the main trunk muscles.

- Second, it wants to keep you alive and fighting, even if you are wounded. Your Reacting Brain minimizes blood loss from wounds by tightening up the blood vessels in your feet, hands, head, and near the surface of the skin because these are the areas where you most likely to be wounded in a fight.

These changes can also contribute to feeling dizzy, unsteady, or faint, and to feeling as if things are 'not quite real' or as if you 'are not fully present.' I explain these feelings next.

Feeling Dizzy, Unsteady, Lightheaded, or Faint

Three factors can make you feel dizzy, unsteady, lightheaded, or faint.

First, changes in blood flow may cause a perceptible, *but harmless*, decrease in blood supply to the brain. Remember, the head is an extremity. It makes sense that the Reacting Brain would send more oxygen to the muscles and less to the brain because you don't need to do a lot of thinking to fight or run for your life.

Sidebar: If you blush when anxious

Anxiety usually increases blood flow to the main fighting muscles and restricts blood flow to the extremities. However, some people have increased blood flow into the face, which causes blushing.

Blushing may be a leftover protective signal that sends a message of apology ("I didn't really mean that! Don't attack me!") or a message of non-threat ("I'm not a threat to you. Don't attack me!").

Recent research shows that people feel warmer and friendlier toward people who blush. So, blushing easily may actually be a good thing!

Second, when you hyperventilate, the imbalance of oxygen and carbon dioxide can make you feel dizzy, lightheaded, etc. Reread the section about Short of Breath and oxygen/carbon dioxide imbalance if you are confused (page 76). This is the most complicated part of the panic response.

Third, the Reacting Brain widens (dilates) the pupils of your eyes in order to expand your field of vision. This makes you more likely to see a predator creeping up on you. However, it can contribute to feeling dizzy, unsteady, lightheaded, or faint and can give you visual changes or feelings of unreality—*all of which are harmless.*

Visual Changes: Blurry, Spots, Dark, Light, etc.

The Reacting Brain makes your pupils larger to expand your field of vision. This helps you spot danger coming and makes you less likely to be ambushed. If there were a real danger, you would find it and instantly focus on it.

Since there is *not* a real danger, you may notice visual changes like things seeming blurry or out of focus. Some people notice spots, tunnel vision (as if the vision is trying to focus in on some danger), or that things seem dark, or too light or bright.

Feeling Unreal or Like You Are Not Present

Four effects of the fight-or-flight response can make you feel as if things are not quite real, or as if you are not really there. This can almost feel like you are having an out-of-body experience and is very common. You <u>are *not* going crazy</u> *nor* are you leaving your body.

Here are the four causes of these feelings.

- The first cause is the vision changes described above. They can make you feel as if things are not real or as if you are viewing things from a distance.

- The second reason for feeling unreal is that your mind and body are both searching for something that is not actually there: they are looking for a threat when you are not actually being threatened. Remember, a panic attack is a fight-or-flight response triggered when there is no actual danger to fight off or flee.

- Third, when the Reacting Brain directs blood to the main muscles and away from extremities, there is a decrease in blood flow to the brain. These changes in blood flow contribute to feeling unreal or feeling like you are not present.

- Fourth, changes in breathing and changes in the oxygen and carbon dioxide balance in the blood also help create these feelings.

The main thing to remember is this: *You are being prepared to deal with danger if it actually occurs.* You can still function.

Also remember: these feelings are temporary. Some people worry that they may "never come back from panic." This does not happen. Panic always decreases eventually.

Nausea, Queasiness, Butterflies or Knots in the Stomach

When your Reacting Brain thinks you are being attacked, it essentially shuts down your digestive system and directs blood and energy to your fighting muscles instead. You cannot run or fight at top speed if you are busy eating or wasting energy digesting.

Shutting down the digestive system can make you nauseous or queasy. It can cause you to lose your appetite. Along with muscle tension, it can give you "butterflies" or "knots" in your stomach.

Think of it this way. If your bodyguard brain thinks you are about to be killed ("You're about to be attacked!"), it is not going to say, "Sit down. Relax. Have a nice meal. Would you like to see the wine list?"

Diarrhea or Vomiting

The same actions that cause nausea and other stomach symptoms can cause diarrhea or make you throw up. Diarrhea and vomiting helped your ancestors survive for the following reasons.

First, if you empty your system, you are lighter and may be able to run faster. Second, if you have diarrhea or you throw up, your smell and taste change in ways that make you unappealing to predators who want to eat you!

It is reassuring to know that even if you throw up when you panic, you can still perform and function. Many famous performers routinely throw up offstage before giving award-winning performances.

Lump in the Throat, Choking, or Can't Swallow

Shutting down your digestive system makes your throat dry. Tensed muscles around the throat can create a feeling of choking, or a feeling of having a lump in your throat. Your airway remains open despite this feeling. You will not choke or suffocate. You will always be able to breathe and swallow no matter how panicky you get.

Here is why. The muscles of the throat are long vertical muscles that move food and liquids down toward the stomach. They are not circular muscles. They cannot tighten shut.

You only choke if something physically blocks your windpipe such as a big piece of unchewed food blocking your airway, someone choking you, or having a severe allergic reaction called anaphylactic shock where the throat tissues swell closed. Panic does not cause choking. In fact, guess what people with life-threatening allergies carry to save their lives by reversing throat tissue swelling? Epinephrine, which is another name for adrenaline!

Do a quick Tight Throat Windpipe Exercise to better understand throat symptoms.

Tight Throat Windpipe Exercise

Press your fingers against the front of your throat, especially the lower part. Do you notice how even a little pressure creates a feeling of choking?

Now, move your fingers up and down and feel around your windpipe. Feel how hard your airway is, and how protected it is.

Because the windpipe is so hard, even slight pressure from tensed muscles outside the throat—especially when combined with dryness inside the throat—can make it feel like there is a lump in your throat or your throat is closing, even when it is not.

The paradox of feeling like something is happening, when it is not, is a repeated theme in panic. You feel as if you cannot breathe or swallow, but you can. You feel like you are not getting enough air, when you are actually breathing in too much. You feel like you are in danger, but you are not.

Feeling like You Cannot Think or Concentrate

You may feel as if you cannot think straight or concentrate during an anxiety attack. You are actually concentrating just fine. The trouble is that you are concentrating on fears, threats, worries, and your panic—not on the issues *you want to concentrate on.*

As you carry out the steps in this book, you will lose your fear of anxiety. Because you no longer fear anxiety, more of your brain will be free to focus on other things.

What If Panic Lasts a Long Time?

There are three reasons why a panic attack can seem to last for a long time:

- First, your sense of time may change as part of the fight-or-flight response. Unpleasant experiences often seem to last longer.

- Second, it takes a while for your adrenaline levels to decline, since you are not running or fighting.

- Third, remaining physically and emotionally ready to fight or flee for a while had survival value because dangers may linger in the wild. If there was one lion, there may be another; it was useful to stay alert for a while.

Panic will go away on its own. However, your tension and anxiety levels may remain high if:

- You have unresolved stresses or other triggers.

- You start to worry about panicking.

- You are worrying about something else.

Any of these make it more likely that your Reacting Brain will respond with more panic attacks and/or keep you chronically tense. We will deal with overcoming these issues later.

Aftereffects

Following a panic attack, you may notice some aftereffects.

Exhaustion, Feeling Tired

Feeling exhausted or tired usually occurs when the danger is over, or after the panic attack ends and the adrenaline wears off. Your body has worked hard to prepare to meet danger. It is tired. This is normal and harmless.

Trouble Sleeping

You may have trouble sleeping after a panic attack if you are frightened by panic or worry about panicking again. Because you are afraid or worried, your devoted—but dumb—caveman Reacting Brain does not want you to let down your guard and go to sleep. It wants you to stay alert. Use this book to help calm your inner bodyguard. Complete a Panic Record and update your Fears vs. Facts form, if necessary.

Chapter Summary

Your fight-or-flight response is amazing and awe-inspiring. Every part of it makes sense—even if it goes off when you do not want or need it. Increasing your understanding of the protective purpose behind every physical change will make these sensations less upsetting.

Form 5-99: Completed Chapter 5

Date completed: _____

Lessons learned:

_____

We have looked at the causes of anxiety or panic sensations, why these sensations may be upsetting, and how they are actually safe. We also discussed why panic attacks may seem to go on forever and reasons why you may feel tired or wired afterwards.

Take a minute to track your progress on Form 5-99: Completed Chapter 5 and note things you have learned, or been surprised by, in this chapter.

Chapter **6:**

Your Fear and Danger Thoughts

"I went to the Emergency Room because I was convinced I was dying."
— John

"I was afraid I was going crazy." — Miriam

"It felt like I was out of control. I didn't know what I might do." — Ann

Let's get in a time machine and return for a moment to the world of your ancestors—the world your Reacting Brain was designed to handle. One day your ancestor goes out for a walk.

The sky is blue. The flowers are blooming. Your ancestor is admiring the scenery and thinking happy thoughts on the way to the watering hole. Meanwhile, the ever-vigilant Reacting Brain is scanning the environment, looking for threats.

Suddenly the Reacting Brain notices danger: a lion ready to pounce, or a snake about to strike! The Reacting Brain instantly pumps out adrenaline, getting the body *physically* ready to run or fight.

But being physically ready doesn't help, if your ancestor doesn't notice the danger. If your ancestor continues to admire the flowers instead of seeing the danger, he or she will become lion lunch or snake snack.

The Reacting Brain must interrupt whatever your ancestor is thinking and change the focus of conscious attention. Since it is a primitive part of the brain, it sends a primitive message.

Here's the message.

Ready?

"DANGER!!!!!!!!!!!!!!!!!!!!!!!!!"

That's it. No details. No specifics. Just an urgent message of danger. Your ancestor immediately reacts, "Danger?!? What danger? Where? Where?" and looks around for danger. Your ancestor sees the danger in time, acts, and survives.

Your Fear and Danger Thoughts

Unusual physical sensations that come 'out of the blue' can be frightening. It is natural to try and figure out what is going on.

Because panic causes bodily sensations, you may worry that something is physically wrong or that you have a medical problem. Because you didn't *decide* to feel this way, you may worry about being out of control or going crazy. What fears do you have about panicking?

Think about your anxiety or panic attacks. What scares you about them?

On Form 6-01: Fear and Danger Thoughts Checklist mark each fear thought that has popped into your mind – even if you know it is not true. If you have other fear thoughts that are not listed, add them in at the end.

Where's the Danger?

When you lived in a world filled with dangerous predators, having this response hard-wired into your brain and body saved your life. When the Reacting Brain found danger, it prepared you – physically, emotionally, and mentally – to look around, find the danger, and flee or fight so you survived.

The problem is, today the same response is activated when your triggers are hit and send a message of any kind of threat, physical or not, real or imagined. Your Reacting Brain pumps out adrenaline and sends a compelling message of "Danger!" – flooding your mind with thoughts of fear and danger.

Form 6-01: Fear and Danger Thoughts Checklist

Mark each fear thought you have experienced. If you have any fear thoughts that are not listed here, add them in at the end:

❑ Anxiety will get worse and worse

❑ Anxiety or panic will never end

❑ Something is medically wrong, like a heart attack, stroke, brain tumor, aneurysm, cancer, or

_____

❑ I will choke, suffocate, be unable to breathe

❑ I will die

❑ I will fall or pass out. If I pass out, I will never wake up

❑ I could be paralyzed by panic and unable to move

❑ Anxiety will damage my mind or my body

❑ I will be unable to think or function, unable to work, unable to care for my family

❑ If I panic while driving, I could crash the car

❑ I am going crazy, having a nervous breakdown, or will "never come back" mentally

❑ I am out of control or could go out of control

❑ I might do something dangerous

❑ I will embarrass myself or my family

❑ Everyone can see when I am anxious

❑ People will think I am weird, crazy, or incompetent; they will judge, criticize, or reject me because of my panic or anxiety

Write down any other fear thoughts you have about panic:

_____

So now, even when it is a false alarm, your body is telling you you're in danger; your emotions are telling you you're in danger; your mind is flooded with thoughts of fear and danger. Naturally, you look around to find the danger you assume is there: "Where? Where is it? Something must be dangerous! Could it be this? What if it's this?"

If you do not understand that your well-intentioned, but misinformed, Reacting Brain *is* raising a false alarm, you will see "danger"—even when it is not there. You may decide that **where you are or what you are <u>doing</u> is dangerous**. Fear and danger thoughts can come to your mind as scary statements, images, or questions.

Here are some common examples of fear thoughts:

- "It feels dangerous to be too far from home, or in a crowd, or alone. What if I can't reach safety or get help?"

- "What if I panic around other people? Everyone will know. They'll think I'm weird, incompetent, or crazy. I will be embarrassed, and it will be horrible."

- "I panicked while driving. If I panic again while driving, I will crash!"

And if you don't see any outside danger threatening you, you may look inside your body and decide that **what is happening <u>inside</u> you is dangerous**:

- "I didn't choose to have this response. I can't stop it. I must be out of control! I might do something dangerous!"

- "My heart's pounding. I have chest pain and tingling; I must be having a heart attack, or a stroke. Or a brain tumor, or an aneurysm. Something is medically wrong!"

- "I'm dizzy; I'm going to pass out."

- "I am going crazy or having a nervous breakdown. I won't be able to function."

- "What if the panic gets worse and worse and never ends?"

- "I can't breathe. I'm suffocating."

- "I can't swallow." "I could become paralyzed."

And so on and so on.

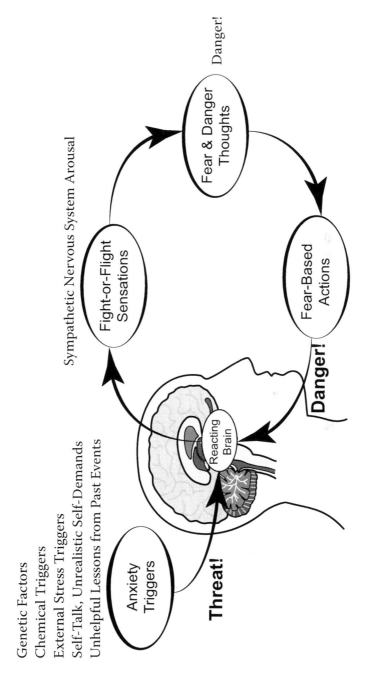

Figure 6-01: Anxiety Leading to Fear and Danger Thoughts

Story: Amanda

Amanda's panic attack at the mall embarrassed her. She was ashamed that she made "such a big deal over nothing!" But she remains scared. It has been two years and she still has not gone back inside the mall. "Believe me, *I have tried*, but every time I even think about the mall I feel dizzy, tingly, and shaky. I have a hard time breathing. What if I got stuck in there and couldn't get outside for fresh air?"

Amanda's main fear is that if she had a panic attack in the mall, she would not be able to breathe and would faint or lose control of herself. She fears the mall—a danger *outside herself*—and she fears her anxiety panic response—a danger *inside herself*.

Your Caveman Brain in Today's World

Your Reacting Brain is essential and can save your life, but it was designed to help your caveman ancestors survive in a different world where threats were physical. In today's modern world, most "dangers" or "threats" are not physical.

The world has changed, but your brain has not. It still has only the one fight-or-flight response to any perceived "danger" or "threat" whether physical or financial, predator or interpersonal, real, remembered, or imagined. So, when your triggers are hit and send a false alarm of danger, your Reacting Brain prepares you physically, emotionally, and mentally to find danger and urges you to run or fight for your life.

Your Reacting Brain bodyguard is *devoted, but dumb*. It is not verbal, not conscious, and not logical. It reacts automatically and unthinkingly to any message of threat.

Its job is to protect you, so it selectively learns and remembers "danger", not safety. And the more feelings, thoughts, situations, activities, or sensations it associates with danger, the more likely it is to misfire to "protect" you. I think of it as being *well-intentioned, but misinformed*.

A misfiring or false alarm in this system is an uncomfortable, unneeded, inconvenient, and miserable experience—*AND it is still the same protective, life-saving response that your body is designed to handle.* Every bodily sensation has a purpose. It is an awe-inspiring, wondrous system, intended to protect you. It is hard-wired and built into you. Too bad it is so stupid.

Now It All Makes Sense!

For the first time, you may understand why your upsetting thoughts and feelings happen. Re-read, review, mark up, and highlight this book until you really understand what happens mentally and physically during anxiety and panic. Think about what you have learned.

In the next chapter (Your Fear-Based Actions), you will learn how certain actions set up a vicious cycle of panic. Later in this book, you will learn how to break free of panic by changing these actions.

Your Fear Thoughts

Review your Form 6-01: Fear and Danger Thoughts Checklist (page 89) and see if there is anything you want to add. Sometimes repeatedly asking 'why something is scary' or 'what might happen' helps uncover deeper fears lurking behind your initial thought. Put into words what your fears are assuming or predicting, as clearly and specifically as possible.

Shortly (in Chapter 8) you will start tracking your panic attacks using Panic Record forms. Use these forms to record your fears and panic thoughts as they come to you.

You may also want to complete Panic Record forms for memorable panic attacks that happened in the past. Completing forms and analyzing past attacks can help you identify all your fears and concerns.

After you have identified your fears, you will learn how to analyze, question, and evaluate them. You will change the way you think about unrealistic fear thoughts.

Form 6-99: Completed Chapter 6

Date completed: _____

Lessons learned:

_____

Chapter Summary

This chapter has covered tools for helping you identify the fear thoughts underlying your anxiety and panic. We have also looked at how your Caveman Brain creates its own version of fears.

Track your progress using Form 6-99: Completed Chapter 6. Note things you have learned, or been surprised by, in this chapter.

Chapter **7:**

Your Fear-Based Actions

"My life was more and more restricted. I started to feel like a prisoner."
— Susan

"Over time my anxiety began to spread, so I started having panic attacks in more places." — Richard

Fear of anxiety or panic can make you change what you do or how you do things. Think about all the ways anxiety affects your life. What do you:

- Do, do differently, do in a special way, or have changed since you started having anxiety or panic, or in order to feel safe?

- No longer do or avoid because you fear anxiety or panic?

Form 7-01: Fear-Based Actions Checklist (page 96) lists things that people with anxiety commonly do, or avoid, because they fear anxiety or panic.

Understanding Your Fear-Based Actions

Let's recap where you are so far in understanding your anxiety cycle. Something has triggered the fight-or-flight response (anxiety trigger). As a result, your body is telling you that you are in danger (fight-or-flight sensations). Your emotions are telling you that you are in danger (fear, anxiety, worry). Your fear thoughts are telling you that you are in danger (fear and danger thoughts). The natural reaction is to believe that you are in danger.

Unless you were taught about panic (and most of us never were), you have no way of knowing that this is a harmless, false alarm. You think something dangerous or threatening is happening when it is not.

Form 7-01: Fear-Based Actions Checklist (1 of 2)

Check all the actions you have taken because of anxiety or panic. If you take actions or avoid activities not listed here, add them on the lines at the end.

Do you:

☐ Call 911 or go to the Emergency Room?

☐ Go to the doctor or ask for medical tests?

☐ Know where the nearest hospital is, just in case?

☐ Take medicine to stop panic attacks?

☐ Always carry medicine with you 'just in case'?

☐ Try to always be with someone?

☐ Go off by yourself to be alone because of panic?

☐ Do other things because panic sensations scare you, such as drink water, eat, hyperventilate, call someone, go outside, open the car windows, turn on the air conditioner, etc.?

Write them here:

_____

_____

_____

_____

_____

_____

Form 7-01: Fear-Based Actions Checklist (2 of 2)

Do you avoid:

☐ Leaving home?

☐ Going very far from home or to unfamiliar places?

☐ Driving alone?

☐ Driving on freeways or in the fast lane?

☐ Bridges, tunnels, or heights?

☐ Work or school?

☐ Parties or social situations?

☐ Crowded situations?

☐ Places you can't leave easily, such as:

- Backseat of car
- Middle of a row or pew
- Elevators or escalators
- Buses, trains, subways, tunnels
- Airplanes
- Dental appointments
- Driving in slow traffic, heavy traffic, or traffic jams
- Other enclosed spaces? Give examples:

_____

Add other activities or situations you avoid or do in a special way to feel safe:

_____

_____

_____

Because you (mistakenly) think that you are in danger, you do what any sane, healthy, sensible person would do. You take actions that would be appropriate and lifesaving, *if a real threat existed*. Unfortunately—in response to a false alarm—the very same actions can make everything worse.

Let us review the five *natural—but mistaken—actions* people take when frightened by anxiety or panic. These actions reduce anxiety in the short term but tend to make anxiety worse over time.

While reading about fear-based actions, think about *what you do* in response to anxiety or panic. Review the actions you identified on Form 7-01: Fear-Based Actions Checklist (page 96).

Panic Action 1: Escape, Leave

One common response to anxiety or panic is to escape physically. You leave the situation, leave the room, leave work or school, leave a meeting, get out of the fast lane, or pull off the road. Maybe you go outside, go home, or go off by yourself.

Or maybe you escape by "leaving mentally." You distract yourself, listen to music, turn on the radio or TV, surf the internet, talk to someone, pray, count, or imagine being in a "safe place."

Do you leave situations, physically or in your mind, because of anxiety or panic? When? How? Make sure to include these actions on your Form 7-01: Fear-Based Actions Checklist.

Panic Action 2: Avoid

A second response to anxiety or panic is to avoid certain activities, situations, people, places, feelings, or thoughts. You are trying to avoid panicking.

It's as if your Reacting Brain is saying, "Man, you dodged *that* bullet, but don't press your luck! What if it happens again? What if it gets worse?" It urges you to *avoid* the "danger" by staying away.

Think about activities or situations you avoid out of fear. Include everything you avoid on your Form 7-01: Fear-Based Actions Checklist.

Panic Action 3: Stay on the Lookout for Danger

A third response is to remain constantly on the lookout for possible signs of danger. "How's my heart? How's my breathing? How's my thinking? Am I sure I'm in control? Am I anxious? Are people looking at me?" and so on. It is as if you are on red alert. You become hypervigilant.

This is a little like what happens after watching an unexpectedly scary movie. While going to the movie, you were relaxed, excited, and happy, "Boy, I heard this is great. Let's get some popcorn." On the way out, you may be jumpy and nervous. The street seems darker. The people you pass look more threatening. Suddenly, the house has all kinds of scary noises. Frightening thoughts leap into your mind. Things you never noticed before now grab your attention and appear threatening.

What happens when you are on the alert and looking for signs of danger? Right! You seem to find them.

Have you begun scanning your body for signs of anxiety? Are you looking for signs of danger around you? What are you finding yourself more nervous about? Add any action you take that involves staying on the lookout for danger to your Form 7-01: Fear-Based Actions Checklist.

Panic Action 4: "Safety Actions"

A fourth common response is to do certain things to keep yourself "safe" from the "danger." I call these "safety actions."

For example, do you:

- Carry water because you fear your throat will close if you don't have something to drink?

- Memorize nearby hospital locations for emergency medical care?

- Stay at home, or close enough to home, so you feel safe?

- Only go to familiar locations?

- Shop only during off-hours or in smaller stores?

- Stay with "safe people"?

- Say prayers for safety?

- Sit only at the end of a row or in the front seat of a car?

- Carry medicine with you at all times, in case you feel anxious?

- Carry a cell phone, not because it is convenient, but in order to get help if you have a panic attack?

The real trouble with safety actions is that your Reacting Brain thinks *these actions* are the reason you survive. These actions *prevent* your brain from learning that the panic was a harmless false alarm, that you were safe all along, and that there was no danger.

What safety actions are you taking? What do you do to keep yourself "safe"? Include "safety" actions on your Form 7-01: Fear-Based Actions Checklist.

Panic Action 5: Fight the Anxiety Response

The final common response is to fight the anxiety response itself because it frightens you. Perhaps you have been telling yourself, "Relax! Relax! Breathe! Breathe!" because you are afraid something terrible will happen if you cannot calm yourself down.

As you have probably found, this does not work very well! Fighting anxiety out of fear is like using gasoline to put out a fire. Being afraid of an anxiety attack and fighting its symptoms—although understandable—often makes things worse. Your Reacting Brain sees you fighting the anxiety response because you are frightened and responds to your fear of panic by pumping out even more adrenaline.

Add any actions you have been taking in a frightened effort to fight, stop, or control panic because you think it could be dangerous to your Form 7-01: Fear-Based Actions Checklist.

Why These Reactions Make Sense

All five of the actions above are appropriate when there is real danger. If it is late at night and you are alone in a dangerous neighborhood, it may save your life to listen for footsteps (stay alert and on the lookout for danger), have a cell phone to call for help (safety action), run if someone starts following you (escape/leave), and fight if attacked (fight). If you survive, it is smart to stay out of similar situations in the future (avoid).

In truly dangerous situations, escaping, avoiding, staying safe, staying on the lookout for threats, and fighting if you have no other choice are the right actions to take. But taking these fear-based actions in response to false alarms creates a vicious cycle.

How These Reactions Make Things Worse

These reactions are all fight actions (fighting the anxiety), flight actions (leave, avoid), or actions that prepare you to fight or flee (look for danger; seek safety). The more fear-based fight-or-flight actions you take, the more likely you are to activate your fight-or-flight response.

Your actions send powerful messages to your Reacting Brain. Your bodyguard Reacting Brain watches what you do. When it sees you take Fear-Based Actions, it concludes, "There must be REAL DANGER, or you wouldn't act that way. I need to save you!"

It remembers where you were, who you were with, and what you were thinking or feeling when you took a panic action. It may decide that any of those things are signs of threat or danger. This, of course, makes it *more likely* to react to any of these in the future. Fear-Based Actions become past events that teach unhelpful lessons and thereby trigger more messages of threat ("this is dangerous").

The *immediate* result of taking fear-based actions (leaving, avoiding, taking safety actions, fighting the anxiety, etc.) is that you feel better. The *longer term and more important result* is that these actions create a vicious cycle by increasing triggers.

Stories: Fear-Based Actions

Story: Carlos

ESCAPE/LEAVE: Carlos loves spending time with his family but when he starts to feel panicky during family gatherings, the first thing he does is try to get away. The idea of having a panic attack around his family is horrifying to Carlos because he believes his family will think he is "weak." Carlos will come up with any excuse to leave situations as fast as possible. This causes tension and hurt feelings because his family doesn't understand why he often leaves gatherings early.

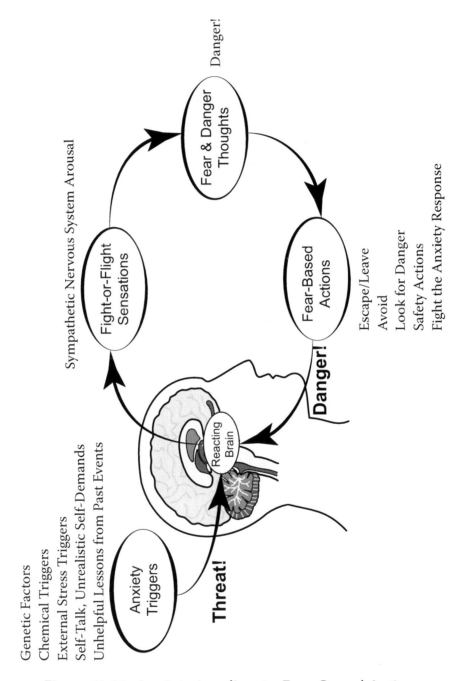

Figure 7-01: Anxiety Leading to Fear-Based Actions

FIGHT THE ANXIETY RESPONSE: Other times Carlos tries to fight the anxiety. He tells himself to "Just relax or you'll have a heart attack!" Carlos believes (wrongly) that if he doesn't calm down quickly, panic will cause a heart attack. You can imagine that yelling at yourself to "just relax!" isn't very relaxing for Carlos, and this frustrates and scares him even more.

Story: Raj

AVOID and SAFETY ACTIONS: When Raj has a panic attack, he sweats, gets nauseous, and has a dry, choking feeling in his throat. His heart races and he feels dizzy. He fears that if he has a panic attack at a social gathering, he might vomit or have diarrhea in front of everyone. He remembers getting food poisoning at the company party and thinks, "What if I hadn't gone home? What if I got sick in front of all my coworkers and my boss? I would be so embarrassed!"

Because of his fear, Raj increasingly avoids events where he may be expected to eat. At first, he just avoided work events, but lately he began avoiding any event where there is food, even gatherings of close friends and family. He wants to be with his friends and family, but fear of panic symptoms stops him.

If his boss forces him to attend a dinner with potential clients, Raj gets very anxious and makes excuses to avoid eating ("I already had dinner," "I had a late lunch," etc.). As a safety action, he always drives his own car, so he can leave in a hurry "just in case."

Story: Amanda

SAFETY ACTION: Shortly after her first panic attack, Amanda went to her doctor for help. The doctor prescribed a fast-acting anti-anxiety medicine to take if she felt anxious. Having the medicine was very reassuring at first. But now Amanda notices that she never leaves home without her pills. If she forgets her pill bottle, she gets scared and immediately goes home for the pills, even if that makes her late for work. She doesn't take pills very often but is frightened to leave home without them. Carrying pills has become a safety action that feeds and supports her anxiety cycle.

Story: Liah

STAY ON THE LOOKOUT FOR DANGER: After entering treatment, Liah realized she was a master at looking out for danger. She is constantly scanning for "anything out of the ordinary." She frequently asks her boyfriend for reassurance that she isn't "having a nervous breakdown" like her mother. Liah told us, "It's like my brain is always watching and waiting for something to go wrong." The panic action of always being on red alert takes a toll on Liah's body, her relationships, and her work performance. "I can never relax because I am always waiting for something bad to happen."

Your Specific Fear-Based Actions

Review your Form 7-01: Fear-Based Actions Checklist and think about other ways you may be leaving, avoiding, looking for danger, taking "safety actions," or fighting the anxiety response. Add these to your checklist. Your list will help you break free of panic.

Chapter Summary

We have discussed five common fear-based actions (escape, avoid, stay on the lookout, "safety actions," and fighting the anxiety response), why these actions make sense, and how these reactions can make things worse. You have reviewed your list of fear-based actions and added any you might have missed.

Track your progress using Form 7-99: Completed Chapter 7. Note things you have learned, or been surprised by, in this chapter.

Form 7-99: Completed Chapter 7

Date completed: _____

Lessons learned: _____

_____

Chapter **8:**

Review Your Anxiety Cycle

*"You gain strength, courage and confidence by every experience in which
you really stop to look fear in the face. You are able to say to yourself, 'I
lived through this…. I can take the next thing that comes along.'"*
– Eleanor Roosevelt

Review your forms and see what you can learn. For example:

- **Amanda:** Filling out these forms helped Amanda identify her *sensations, fears* and *actions*. Her *sensations* include feeling dizzy, shortness of breath, choking sensation, feeling numb and tingly, and shaking. Her *fears* include suffocating, passing out, and losing control. Due to these sensations and fears, her *actions* include avoiding crowded places, especially the mall.

- **Raj:** Forms helped Raj identify his *sensations* (stomach discomfort/nausea, dizziness, sweating, racing heart, and a dry choking sensation in his throat), his *fears* (having diarrhea/vomiting in public, eating in public, and being embarrassed) and his *actions* (avoiding eating in public and driving his own car to social events so he can leave quickly if his stomach gets upset).

- **Liah:** Liah used her forms to identify her *sensations* (heart racing, chills, sweating, trembling, feeling disconnected from her body, and feeling like she can't breathe), her *fears* (having a nervous breakdown, going crazy, not being in control of herself), and her *actions* (telling herself to "calm down!", opening the windows in the car, and drinking cold water).

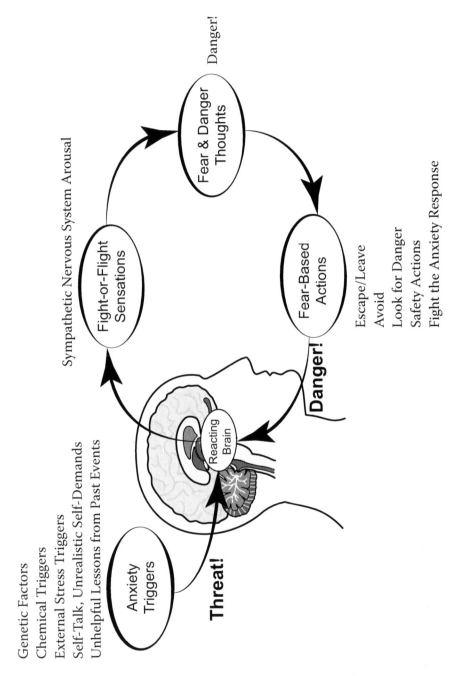

Figure 8-01: Complete Anxiety Model

- **Carlos**: Carlos' forms helped him identify his *sensations* (fast heartbeat, chest pain or pressure, sweating, hot flashes, and a choking sensation in his throat), his *fears* (dying, having a heart attack or some other serious medical disease or physical problem, others seeing his anxiety and thinking he is weak), and his *actions* (telling himself to "relax or you'll have a heart attack!", going to the doctor, and abruptly leaving family gatherings if he feels panicky).

Check Your Understanding

Check your understanding of the anxiety cycle by completing Form 8-01: Anxiety Cycle Review.

If you do not agree with any of the statements in the review form:

- Try rereading the previous chapters and see if they make more sense.

- Look at the contents of Chapter 14: Problems and Solutions and read any topics that are relevant for you.

- If you are seeing a therapist or healthcare provider, ask them for help answering your questions.

- If you are not working with a therapist or healthcare provider, and are still confused after reviewing this material, consider finding a therapist. See the Appendix for more information.

Form 8-01: Anxiety Cycle Review

☐ What I have read so far makes logical sense to me.

☐ It helps explain why I have anxiety or panic attacks.

☐ It explains the purpose of my anxiety or panic sensations.

☐ It helps explain my fears and panic thoughts.

☐ I see how each part of the cycle makes anxiety continue.

Start Charting

Now that you understand your anxiety cycle, I will help you learn how to change it, overcome your anxiety, and break free of fear. The best way to learn this is by tracking your experience and progress.

Recording your sensations, thoughts, and actions helps you identify:

- Patterns, so anxiety/panic makes more sense and feels less unpredictable;

- Anxiety or panic sensations, including those you have most often, or that scare you the most, so you can learn more about them;

- Fear and danger thoughts, and put them into words so your logical Thinking Brain can begin to take over;

- Fear-based actions so you can change what you do and break your cycle of anxiety.

We provide Anxiety Records for daily/weekly tracking, and Panic Records for each attack, as explained below.

Anxiety Record

Anxiety Records help you see daily or weekly anxiety patterns and track your progress as you overcome your anxiety. They can also help you recognize and savor things that are going well in your life.

At the end of each day take a few minutes to update your Anxiety Record.

Using paper forms: fill out Form 8-02 Anxiety Record (page 110), completing the entries for the current day and adding the summary at the end of each week, per the instructions below.

Paper Form Instructions

Update this form every day and complete the summary at the bottom on the last day of each week.

1. Record how many anxiety episodes you had during the day. This includes full or partial panic attacks.

2. Rate your *overall anxiety level* for the day on a scale of 0-10. Anxiety includes feelings like worry, fear, stress, or tension.

3. Rate your *average* level of *worry about having another episode of panic* on a scale of 0-10.

4. Add a comment about the day or note 'good things' that happened and why (see below).

5. Optional: if you are menstruating, number the days starting when you get your period to track where you are in your monthly cycle.

At the end of each week complete the bottom part of the Anxiety Record:

1. **Add up** the total number of anxiety episodes for the week. Write down that number.

2. **Add** your Overall Daily Anxiety Level numbers to get a total for the week. **Then divide the total** by 7 to get an *Average* Daily Anxiety *for the week*. (If you did not record every day, divide the total by the number of days on which you did record. For example, if you have ratings for 6 days, divide the total by 6.)

3. **Add** your Overall Daily Worry about Panic numbers to get a total for the week. **Then divide the total** by 7 to get an **Average** Overall Daily Worry about Panic *for the week*. (If you did not record every day, divide the total by the number of days on which you did record. For example, if you have ratings for 6 days, divide the total by 6.)

4. **List three good things** that happened during the week and a few words about why each happened.

Panic Record

Whenever you have a panic attack or a surge of fear or anxiety, fill out Form 8-03: Panic Record (page 114) as soon as possible. This will help you get the facts about your panic and your anxiety cycle.

This form will help you identify any *bodily sensations* that still scare you. Using the form also helps you uncover *fear thoughts* of danger or threat, including fears that may flash through your mind so quickly that you are not aware of them at the time. Capturing fear thoughts, and putting them into words, will allow your Thinking Brain to begin to take over. Writing down

Form 8-02: Anxiety Record

Anxiety Record for the week of _____
Use this 10-point scale for the overall ratings:

```
0------1------2------3------4------5------6------7------8------9-------10
None        Mild          Moderate        Strong      Extreme
```

Day	Number of Anxiety Episodes	Overall Anxiety Level (0-10)	Worry about Panic (0-10)	Comments
Mon				
Tue				
Wed				
Thu				
Fri				
Sat				
Sun				
Total				
Average				
Three Good Things/ Why				

Calculate averages by dividing the Total by the number of days
for which you have ratings (typically 7).

each *action* you take when you feel panicky helps you change fear-based actions that strengthen and maintain your anxiety cycle.

In the bottom part of the Panic Record, review each episode in slow motion. Think like a detective reconstructing a crime and ask what happened at each step. Solve the mystery of *why and how* your Reacting Brain thought it had to save you. What do you guess your caveman brain thought might happen?

Another way to think about this is like being the coach of a sports team. A coach videos each game and reviews the plays in slow motion, analyzing what went right and what went wrong at every step. You can do the same. Play back each episode in your memory and analyze it.

Write down every sensation, every thought, and every action from just before you got anxious until the end. At each step, ask "And then, what did I feel? What did I think? What did I do?" Explore each brief, fleeting thought and put it into words. Guess what might have been worrying your Reacting Brain. See how your body, thoughts, and actions affect each other.

The more information you get, the smarter you become at overcoming panic. These forms will help you identify which sensations you need to learn more about, which fear thoughts you need to talk back to, and which actions you need to change. The more effort you put into these records, the more they will help you. I recommend using the forms daily until you have achieved your personal goal.

Panic Happens Less Than Once a Week

Perhaps you worry about panic but do not actually have full or partial panic attacks very often. Fill out the Anxiety Record daily as recommended. When you do have a full or partial panic attack or surge of anxiety, fill out a Panic Record.

In weeks when you do *not* have any anxiety or panic episodes, fill out Panic Records based on your memory of past panic attacks and fear episodes. The purpose of these records is to help you understand how your sensations, thoughts, and actions interact and what you can change to break your anxiety cycle.

Example Anxiety Record: Amanda Week 1

Anxiety Record for the week of _____June 25_____
Use this 10-point scale for the overall ratings:

```
0------1------2------3------4------5------6------7------8------9-------10
None        Mild           Moderate        Strong        Extreme
```

Day	Number of Anxiety Episodes	Overall Anxiety Level (0-10)	Worry about Panic (0-10)	Comments
Mon	2	5	5	Busy day at work
Tue	1	4	4	Daughter is sick
Wed	4	7	10	Saw ex-husband
Thu	3	8	9	Tried to go to the mall
Fri	1	4	5	Mom being judgmental
Sat	0	2	1	Relaxing day
Sun	1	3	3	Wish could shop at mall
Total	12	33	37	
Average		4.7	5.3	
Three Good Things/ Why	Daughter was only sick briefly because she is generally healthy. Ex-husband was sympathetic, he seems more mature. Church choir was fun, everyone worked together.			

Calculate averages by dividing the Total by the number of days for which you have ratings (typically 7).

Example Anxiety Record: Amanda Week 2

Anxiety Record for the week of __*July 2*_____
Use this 10-point scale for the overall ratings:

0------1------2------3------4------5------6------7------8------9-------10
None   Mild   Moderate   Strong   Extreme

Day	Number of Anxiety Episodes	Overall Anxiety Level (0-10)	Worry about Panic (0-10)	Comments
Mon				*Forgot to rate today*
Tue	*1*	*5*	*4*	*Preparing for family*
Wed	*3*	*5*	*6*	*Family gathering*
Thu	*3*	*4*	*6*	*Daughter is fussy*
Fri	*1*	*3*	*3*	*Regular work day*
Sat				*Forgot to rate today*
Sun	*1*	*2*	*1*	*Relaxing day*
Total	*10*	*19*	*20*	
Average		*3.8*	*4.0*	
Three Good Things/ Why	*Family gathering was fun because everyone helped out. Work has been good because coworkers are more considerate. Really enjoyed church service, could just relax and listen.*			

Calculate averages by dividing the Total by the number of days
for which you have ratings (typically 7).

Form 8-03: Panic Record

Date/time: _____ Duration: _____ Level (0-10): _____

Check all that apply:

- ❑ Fast/pounding heart
- ❑ Chest pain/tightness
- ❑ Short of breath
- ❑ Sweaty/Hot/Cold
- ❑ Tingling/numb
- ❑ Stomach/GI feelings
- ❑ Dizzy/lightheaded
- ❑ Feel unreal
- ❑ Vision changes
- ❑ Trembling/shaky/weak
- ❑ Choking feeling
- ❑ Other: _____

Fears:

- ❑ Suffocate/pass out
- ❑ Medical problem/die
- ❑ Crazy/Lose control
- ❑ Panic never end
- ❑ Other: _____

Actions:

- ❑ Escape/Leave
- ❑ Avoid
- ❑ Look for danger
- ❑ Safety actions
- ❑ Fight the anxiety response

What was your first sign of panic? A sensation? A thought? An action?

_____

Next sensation, thought, or action?

_____

Then what did you think, do, or feel?

_____

Then what?

_____

Then what?

_____

Preparing to Break Free

Once you have a good understanding of your anxiety cycle, move to the next section and start changing your cycle to break free of anxiety. Continue to chart using the Anxiety and Panic Records.

If you are not sure you understand your anxiety cycle, spend a week charting to gather more information. Complete an Anxiety Record every day and Panic Records for each attack. At the end of the week, review your records and look for patterns and clues. What sensations do you need to understand? What fears do you need to disprove, or thoughts do you need to challenge? What actions do you need to change? What is triggering or maintaining your panic and anxiety cycle? If you identify new triggers, anxiety or panic sensations, fears or danger thoughts, or fear-based actions, add them to the appropriate lists. The information from these forms will help you overcome anxiety and panic.

In the next section, I guide you through the process of breaking this vicious cycle and freeing yourself from anxiety and panic as shown in Figure 8-02 (page 118).

You will learn how to:

- Reduce your anxiety triggers so your Reacting Brain receives fewer messages of threat and these messages are less intense.

- Change your response to anxiety or panic sensations so that you can understand and tolerate these sensations.

- Change your thinking to challenge your fear and danger thoughts, get the facts to identify false alarms, act on the facts, and use coping plans for true alarms.

- Learn that anxiety sensations are safe by repeatedly practicing exercises that cause similar physical changes.

- Learn that activities are safe by deliberately facing fear-inducing activities and situations in a controlled manner.

Keep filling out your Anxiety Record every day and Panic Record forms as needed while you complete the learning process. The information from these forms will help with all the remaining steps.

Example Panic Record: Carlos

Date/time: _7/15 3 p_   Duration: _15_   Level (0-10): _8_

Check all that apply:

☑ Fast/pounding heart	❑ Dizzy/lightheaded
☑ Chest pain/tightness	❑ Feel unreal
☑ Short of breath	❑ Vision changes
☑ Sweaty/Hot/Cold	❑ Trembling/shaky/weak
❑ Tingling/numb	❑ Choking feeling
❑ Stomach/GI feelings	❑ Other: _____

Fears:

❑ Suffocate/pass out	❑ Panic never end
☑ Medical problem/die	❑ Other: _____
❑ Crazy/Lose control	

Actions:

❑ Escape/Leave	☑ Safety actions
❑ Avoid	❑ Fight the anxiety response
❑ Look for danger	

What was your first sign of panic? A sensation? A thought? An action?

Sensation: My heart suddenly started racing.

Next sensation, thought, or action?
Thought: What if this is a heart attack?

Then what did you think, do, or feel?
Sensation: Heart beat even faster. I felt like I couldn't swallow, like I was choking.

Then what?
Thought: I'm dying! I can't breathe. Who will take care of my family?

Then what?
Action: Called for my wife

Example Panic Record: Carlos (continued)

Then what?

Sensation: I was sweaty, cold, dizzy, and had pain in my chest.

Then what?

Thought: This is it. This is definitely a heart attack. I'm going to die.

Then what?

Action: I held my chest and laid down on the bed next to the phone in case I needed to call 911.

Then what?

Action: My wife came in from outside. I listened when she told me that this was a panic attack, not a heart attack. I remembered my other panic attacks caused the same sensations and started to believe her.

Then what?

Thought: Maybe it's just panic.

Then what?

Action: I did belly breathing and reminded myself of what the doctor said and what I had learned about panic.

Then what?

Sensation: After a few minutes, my sensations went back to normal.

Then what?

Then what?

Then what?

Then what?

Then what?

Then what?

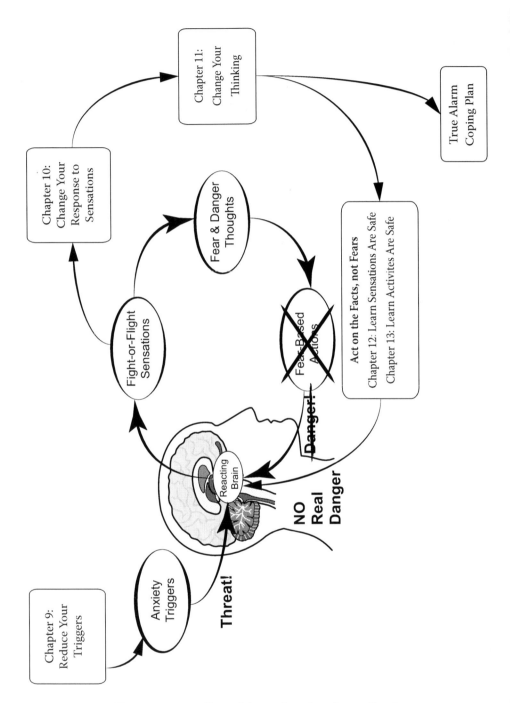

Figure 8-02: Breaking the Anxiety Cycle

Step 2, reducing your anxiety triggers, may take some time and effort, but it also can have huge benefits for every area of your life. If triggers are not a major issue for you, you can do Step 3 first and return to Step 2 later.

Chapter Summary

This chapter focused on understanding your personal anxiety cycle. You also started charting with daily anxiety records and panic records to better understand your anxiety cycle and track changes.

Track your progress using Form 8-99: Completed Chapter 8. Note things you have learned, or been surprised by, in this chapter.

If you have worked through chapters 3 to 8, you have completed Step 1, the longest step in our process. Congratulations! Check Form 1-03: Reward Plan (page 16) to see how you planned to reward yourself for completing this step.

Form 8-99: Completed Chapter 8

Date completed: _____

Lessons learned: _____

_____

Section **2:**

Changing Your Anxiety Cycle

"I had some panic, but I followed your suggestions and quickly squelched the unwanted sensations. Subsequent panic attacks were lower in intensity." – Kayla

"Things that used to be hair-raising are now no big deal." – Jose

"I have a lot more tools. Thank you for showing me what to do.
— Victoria

By now you should have a much better understanding of panic and your own personal cycle of anxiety. You may see how your anxiety triggers, anxiety or panic sensations, fear and danger thoughts, and fear-based actions have been interacting to create and strengthen the anxiety cycle.

Mapping your personal anxiety cycle shows what you need to change. In this section of the book I explain *how* to make those changes effectively. So, roll up your sleeves and get ready for some exciting work!

Chapter 9

Step 2 Reduce Your Triggers

"I told myself: 'You're ready for this. You can do this'." — Paul

"I'm doing really good now. I didn't think it would work, but I believe it now. I was living in fear and now I'm really happy. I still get symptoms sometimes, but they don't bother me. I understand what's happening."
— Lakeesha

In step 2, you reduce your anxiety triggers. Panic may be unexpected, but it is not unreasonable. Identifying what triggers your anxiety and panic (as you did in the earlier chapters) allows you to focus on reducing those triggers. Fewer triggers means fewer false alarms, less panic, less anxiety, and less stress overall.

This chapter covers all the triggers described in Chapter 3 Your Anxiety Triggers. You may only want to read about your specific triggers based on the forms you completed in Chapter 3.

Reduce the Impact of Genetic Factors

Our genes determine many of our physical characteristics. Our height, eye color, skin color, and hair color are inherited. In the same way, our nervous system is inherited. Vulnerability to anxiety or panic can run in families.

If you listed multiple people on Form 3-01: Relatives with Anxiety (page 45), you may have inherited this vulnerability. Recognizing this can motivate you to learn good coping skills. You need to handle panic more skillfully and work harder to reduce any other anxiety triggers than someone without a genetic tendency to anxiety.

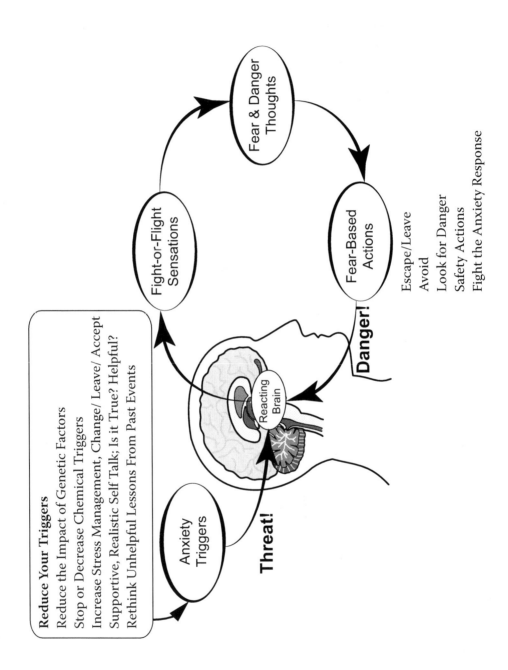

Figure 9-01: Reduce Your Triggers

Think of it as the difference between driving a sports car and a minivan. The sports car responds quickly and intensely to even a light touch on the accelerator; the minivan takes much more time and effort to speed up. You may have inherited a sports-car-type nervous system. You are a Porsche.

Knowing that anxiety runs in your family can help explain why you tend to get anxious. A genetic vulnerability does not mean you will automatically have problems, but it does mean you want to be smart about anxiety. Reading this book is an excellent place to start.

Story: Amanda

Amanda was relieved to learn that anxiety can run in families. "I used to think something was wrong with *me*. Now I realize it is just part of my genetic makeup and I can learn skills to cope with it."

Reduce Chemical Triggers

Legal Stimulants

If you have any tendency to have anxiety, I strongly encourage you to not drink 'energy drinks' and to limit your caffeine intake to the equivalent of 1-2 cups of coffee per day. I am not saying to avoid all caffeine. Different people have different tolerances for caffeine. Just be aware that caffeine may contribute to anxiety sensations by getting your body revved up and ready to react—especially in larger quantities.

Story: Liah

Liah was drinking a lot of coffee because of her demanding schedule. As she started treating her panic, she gradually decreased her coffee until she was down to one cup in the morning. "For me, cutting down the caffeine made a big difference. I was a lot less 'wound up' during the day and could handle the stress better. I also got better, deeper sleep and woke up feeling more rested and relaxed." She made other changes as well, which you will read about as you follow her through the learning process.

Alcohol, Drugs, Medicines, Tobacco

Caution: if you use alcohol, street drugs, or prescription medication daily or in large amounts, talk to your healthcare provider before stopping. Sudden withdrawal can be dangerous.

If you only drink very moderately, try stopping all alcohol for several weeks while carrying out the steps outlined in this book. Notice whether you feel better and less anxious. If you have any concerns about stopping alcohol, talk with your healthcare provider first.

If you have trouble not drinking, consider whether you may have a drinking problem. People without a drinking problem can stop if they choose.

If you have been using street drugs or any form of marijuana (see page 45) for anxiety, I encourage you to consider gradually decreasing and stopping while completing the program in this book. If you have been heavily using street drugs, talk to a healthcare provider or drug counselor about avoiding withdrawal. If you can't stop, or feel you can't cope without these drugs, talk to your healthcare provider or therapist.

If you think prescription medication contributes to your anxiety symptoms, talk to the healthcare provider who is managing your medications. Ask about alternatives and follow their instructions for changing your medication.

If you smoke cigarettes, use tobacco in other forms, or vape, improving your anxiety may be one more reason to stop. Stopping tobacco is one of the best things you can do for your overall health. Ask your healthcare provider about options. Smokefree.gov (http://smokefree.gov) provides free information and professional assistance to help people quit smoking.

Female Hormone Changes

Changing hormone levels can make panic more likely. By tracking the day of your monthly cycle on your daily Anxiety Record, you can see whether (and when) hormone changes affect your level of anxiety level or your likelihood to panic. Many women find they are more emotionally reactive during the week before their period. If this is true for you, keep track of where you are in your cycle and during those days, remind yourself to step back and think, not just react based on your emotions.

Talk to your gynecologist, primary care provider, or psychiatrist if mood swings, anger, or depression due to hormone changes are a problem for you. Sometimes medication can help.

Reduce External Stress Triggers

Look over your list of stresses on Form 3-03: External Stress List (page 49). Think about any unresolved problems in your life and changes you need to make.

Anxiety can be sending a message that you need to change something. Rather than fearing your anxiety, *listen to it.* Try to decode its message to you. What stress triggers do you need to reduce?

Choose Your Response

You can respond to an external stress in four different ways—and only the first three are any good. You can:

1. Change

2. Leave

3. Accept

4. Stay Upset

Change

What can you change to reduce stress in your life? Focus on things that are *under your control.* You control what you say, what you do, whom you spend time with, what you agree to do, what you tell yourself, how you think about things, where you focus your attention, and so on.

Do not focus on things that you do not or cannot control. Remind yourself that you do not control other people's actions, reactions, attitudes, or choices. You do not control what others do or say. You do not control what people think, or how they feel or react.

Alcoholics Anonymous has a wonderful saying that relates to this: "What other people think about me… is none of my business!" Let others worry about their own reactions and choices; you focus on yours.

Leave

After you have changed everything you can to reduce stress, consider whether the best option is to leave a situation. Sometimes panic is trying to send you an important message: "Get out of this stressful or dangerous situation!"

For example, Anna came in for panic treatment because she had begun having panic attacks on her way to work. Reviewing her anxiety triggers, she realized the panic attacks had started after she and her coworkers had been robbed at gunpoint several times. At that point, I told her, "Your anxiety is trying to tell you something important. Listen to it. You do not need panic treatment. You need a safer job!"

Similarly, after Dolores filled out her Anxiety and Panic Records and thought about her triggers, she realized that her panic attacks began after she let her verbally abusive, drug-addicted adult son move in with her. She knew he was dealing drugs from her apartment and was stealing from her. Her panic was trying to tell her she needed to have him move out.

If you are being harassed or targeted at work, or in your neighborhood, if you are being abused or threatened, or if you are in a situation everyone agrees is dangerous or stressful, your best choice may be to leave.

Accept

> *"When faced with the inevitable, you always have a choice. You may not*
> *be able to alter reality, but you can alter your attitude toward it."*
> *– Margaret Atwood*

As the Serenity Prayer puts it, "God grant me the serenity to accept the things I cannot change, courage to change the things I can, and wisdom to know the difference."

Look at your list of external stresses (page 49). If you have changed everything you can, and if you cannot (or choose not to) leave, your only good choice is to truly accept things as they are at this time.

Life brings challenges and losses to each of us. You or your family members may have chronic health problems. You may have money problems or have lost your job or your home. You may have loved ones who are making terrible life choices.

Sometimes acceptance is your best—or only—choice. Acceptance is the healthiest response to bad things you can neither change nor leave.

Please understand I am not saying that you must approve or enjoy what is happening. Nor am I urging you to be a passive victim. Actively change everything you can. Consider leaving. But I know there are times when changing is ineffective and leaving is impossible. When in such a situation, acceptance helps you cope and makes stress less stressful.

What cannot be changed must be accepted. You may not have any other good choices. You may hope that things improve with time, but at the present, as the saying goes, "It is what it is."

Stay Upset

Choice Four, Staying Upset, is common, tempting, and a *really, really bad option*. It involves saying or thinking things like, "The world should not be this way! People shouldn't do/say/think/feel this. It's not right! It's not fair! I hate it! I can't stand it! It's awful and terrible and I'm just going to stay upset about it until it changes!"

Just to be clear: you may have every right to be stressed and unhappy. The situation may be unjust, disappointing, even tragic. The problem is that being upset changes nothing.

Staying upset is like beating your head against a brick wall to make it go away. The brick wall doesn't move; you end up with a bloody head.

Acknowledge that you are stressed, upset, or unhappy. Let your feelings out by writing or talking.

But then step back and think. Decide what you can *change*, whether you will *leave*, and what you have to *accept*. Then act on your decisions.

Anger or anxiety can give you the energy and motivation to change a bad situation. This is good and helpful.

Staying angry, upset, resentful, or anxious is not good or helpful. In fact, it harms your physical and emotional health.

Do not feed your own distress. You deserve better. In a bad situation, your task is to minimize the emotional pain caused by external stress—not increase it through your reaction.

Good Stress Management

Stress management will help you get through hard times and can include physical, mental, spiritual, social, or other activities. Below you will find a list of stress reducers many people find helpful.

Which of these do you practice? Which can you add to your life?

Physical stress reducers: sports, exercise, yoga, tai chi, qi gong, dance, singing, gardening, muscle relaxation, and diaphragmatic or belly breathing (see page 147).

Sleep hygiene: establish healthy sleep habits. Keep your bedroom dark, cool, and quiet. Go to bed at the same time each night. Limit daytime napping to 40 minutes or less. Keep bed for sleeping, relaxing, or sex. Avoid stimulants (such as caffeine, alcohol or nicotine), exercising, or eating close to bedtime.

Mental or spiritual stress reducers: mindfulness, reading, meditation, prayer, or other spiritual practices.

Social stress reducers: spending time with family or friends, talking to people, going to your church, temple, mosque, or club, getting support from close friends or loved ones.

Other stress reducers: anything that makes you feel better (and is not harmful) such as helping others, volunteering, healthy fun activities, activities that use your unique skills and strengths, or other activities that have meaning and value for you.

Examples of Reducing External Stress Triggers

While working a medical center, I helped many people with chronic medical conditions overcome panic. Let us take diabetes as an example of using the four response options to deal with an external stress trigger.

Leave: Leaving is not really an option. You can't just wake up one morning and say, "Today I won't have diabetes."

Change actions that you control: You can exercise more, be more active, make healthier food choices, take your medications regularly, and monitor your blood sugar (glucose) levels. You manage your condition to minimize its impact on your health and reduce your chances of complications.

Change your thinking: Changing how you think and talk to yourself about diabetes lets you consider the lifestyle changes you want to make in ways that are realistic, supportive, and helpful. For example, you can take pride in how well you care for your health. You can focus on other areas of your life that are going well. You can see this as an opportunity to make positive changes and to serve as a role model for others.

Accept: You acknowledge that you have diabetes and accept the need to actively manage your health even though it can be inconvenient.

Stay Upset: You can stay upset about having diabetes. You think about the potential bad outcomes, the restrictions and demands, the unfairness of it all. Staying upset makes you angry, resentful, sad, scared, and/or ineffective.

Story: Raj

Raj knew his long commute was an external stress. At first, he was tempted to "Stay Upset" about it which was understandable. Driving in traffic every day is not fun for most people. But he realized staying upset didn't help.

Then he considered "Leaving" but that would have meant quitting his job. He loved the job and wanted to stay. Plus, there were very few other jobs in his specialty and his family needed his income.

After considering his choices, Raj decided on a combination of "Change" and "Accept". He accepted that he would need to spend at least part of his day commuting. He also made some changes. He got permission to change his work hours on Tuesday through Thursday, so he drove during times when traffic was lighter. Monday and Friday, he started commuting by bus and used the time to read and relax on his way to and from work. After a few weeks, he commented, "I feel less anxious now and I'm noticing that my body is more relaxed."

Reduce Negative Self-Talk and Unrealistic Self-Demands

Why Self-Talk Matters

Self-talk is another word for thinking and thinking and feelings influence each other. For example, when you talk or think about a sad event, you feel sad. When you feel sad, your mind automatically starts remembering and thinking about sad things.

When you are scared, you tend to think scary thoughts, like assuming something bad is happening—or about to happen. You quickly jump to false conclusions about what to expect and whether you can cope. Such thoughts can be vividly convincing even when they are not true.

Thoughts create emotions, emotions bring thoughts to mind, and so on and on. This can either create a positive cycle (more calm, confidence, and coping) or a negative cycle (more panic, anxiety worry, and more fear actions like avoiding or looking for danger).

Self-talk is not only what you think and say to yourself inside your head. It is also the words you use when talking to other people about yourself or about situations.

And the really important point to remember is: *Self-talk is like programming for the Reacting Brain.* The words you use are important because your primitive Reacting Brain takes them *literally.*

If you say or think something is "awful", "terrible", or "a disaster", or that you "can't stand it", "can't cope", or "are drowning" in work, your Reacting Brain believes you. It takes you seriously, it decides that you are in trouble, and you need its help. Consequently, it becomes more likely to trigger panic as a response.

At the level of your conscious Thinking Brain *you know* you don't really mean those words literally. Your caveman Reacting Brain *does not understand* this. It doesn't understand subtleties like metaphors or using exaggeration for effect. It believes you mean precisely what you say – and reacts based on that belief. Remember, it is devoted, but dumb; well-intentioned, but misinformed.

Reduce Negative Self-Talk Triggers

> *"Until I started listening to myself, I didn't realize how hard I was on myself." — Mary*

Review your list of self-talk triggers on Form 3-04: Negative Self-Talk Checklist (page 51). If you are like most people, you may say things and talk to yourself in a way that you would not speak to a friend.

Listen to yourself. Do you *criticize yourself* or *call yourself names* ("stupid idiot")? Do you *predict the worst* or say things will be *awful* ("You'll probably mess up and embarrass yourself. What if you fail? What a disaster!" or "I just know I will panic, and I hate panic! Panic is the most terrible thing in the entire world!")?

Thinking about unpleasant or difficult experiences as "terrible", "horrible", "awful", "torture" and so on is called *catastrophizing*. You focus on the negative aspects of the situation and lose sight of the larger perspective.

Do you talk as if bad things *"always happen"* or you'll *"never learn"* to overcome problems like panic? Does your self-talk say things about other people using negative, all-or-nothing terms (*"No one* else gets anxious or panicky"; *"Everyone* knows something's wrong and thinks I'm weird.")?

When something does not go well, do you put *all* the blame on yourself ("That was *all my fault*") without looking for other contributing factors? Do you talk as if nothing can be changed ("This is just how I am. I'm a loser.")?

Reduce Unrealistic Self-Demands Triggers

> *"I feel like I always have to keep it together for everyone"* — James

> *"Everybody relies on me to save them and to make things right. I feel guilty if I say no. But I'm getting tired of it!"* — Pat

Look at your list of self-demands Form 3-05: Unrealistic Self-Demands Checklist (page 52). When you feel you *must* do something that is impossible or not under your control, you become more stressed and anxious.

Think about what you expect of yourself. Are your demands unrealistic? Would you tell someone you love to make those demands of themselves?

Are you demanding ideal behavior from yourself – or from others? Or are you making unrealistic demands of life, looking for certainty, total safety, or a perfectly fair and just world?

Stop and truly think about the reality that total perfection, perfect control, guaranteed safety, and absolute certainty are all impossible– *and always have been.*

Take a moment and really absorb the truth of that. They are impossible and the more you strive for an impossible goal, the more panicky, worried, angry, and/or depressed you will be.

Uncertainty and imperfection are part of life. Despite this, people through-out the course of human history have lived happy, satisfying lives. Accepting and recognizing this reality helps lessen unrealistic self-demands.

Realistic, Supportive Self-Talk and Self-Demands

Now look at your Form 6-01: Fear and Danger Thoughts Checklist (page 89). How many involve jumping to negative conclusions ("I am going crazy." "I'm having a heart attack." "I'm out of control.") or negative predic-tions ("I will pass out." "Panic will never end." "I will start screaming.")? How many involve catastrophizing ("Panic is unbearable! It is the worst thing in the world!" "I can't stand it." "It's horrible, terrible, awful.")?

The messages you send to yourself, the words you use, and your self-demands should be both *realistic* and *supportive*.

Talk to yourself the way you would talk to your best friend or a beloved child. Be realistic and practical. Be supportive and loving.

Is it True? Is it Helpful?

Here is a quick way to evaluate your self-talk. Listen to what you say either aloud or silently to yourself. Then ask two types of questions:

1. First ask, "Is what I am saying actually, literally 100% proven *true*? What are the *facts*? How true or likely is this *really*? Is it true for *everyone*? Does everyone else see it this way?"

2. Second, ask yourself, "Even if it *is* true, is it *helpful* to say or think this? How bad is this *really*? How can I *cope*? How might *other people* cope and think about this?"

When healthy self-talk is examined in this way ("Is what I'm thinking or saying completely true?" and "Is what I am thinking or saying helpful?"), the answer to both questions is "Yes."

If the answer to **either question** could be "No," change what you are saying.

Your self-talk needs to be *true* <u>and</u> *helpful*.

Carla's Story

Carla joined our panic therapy group but found herself procrastinating, avoiding, and giving up. She would look at this book and think, "I'm too scared to read about anxiety. It will make me worse. The treatment is too hard and I'm sure it won't work for me. Besides, I know I can never do it."

After I encouraged her to question her thoughts, she began to ask, "Do I know these thoughts are guaranteed to be true? Do others believe these ideas? Do these thoughts help me?"

She realized "I can't predict the future, so I don't know for certain what will happen. And I don't know what I can do until I try. I don't know for sure that this treatment will help me, but many other people have done it and been helped. I know it can't help me if I don't even try, so that thinking isn't helpful. If I do get anxious, well, I've been dealing with anxiety for years, so I know it won't kill me and maybe if I keep reading, I will feel better. I survived my life so far, so I know I can cope. Other people believe this treatment really works. It is used around the world because it is so effective."

After questioning her thoughts, she decided to start reading, do what the book suggested, and see where that took her, instead of giving up. By the end of treatment, she was one of our most successful and enthusiastic group members.

Healthy Programming

Most people with self-talk triggers have used negative words and made negative statements for years without noticing the impact of their words. Negative self-talk may become so automatic that you are not even aware of it, until you start listening for it.

Thoughts are discussed in more detail in Chapter 11: Change Your Thinking. In the meantime, see the quick guide in the sidebar Changing Unhelpful Self-Talk (page 137). It gives you examples of how to replace negative self-talk with helpful self-talk.

Try an experiment. Listen carefully to your words and thoughts. Then deliberately, consciously, change the words you use. Replace:

- Negative words that increase stress and anxiety with words that are accurate and realistic, that are supportive, and that encourage coping, balanced thinking, and problem solving.

- Overly general words like "always", "never", "everyone", or "no one" with words that are more specific, more accurate, and more hopeful, like "sometimes", "right now", "not yet", "this specific person", "some people", etc.

Notice how you feel as a result. With practice, helpful thinking becomes easier, more natural, and more automatic.

Story: Liah

Liah used this technique to challenge her critical self-talk. Her reaction at first was, "This sounds really dumb, but I'm willing to try anything at this point."

After a few weeks, Liah reported, "I've gotten really good at noticing my negative self-talk and changing it. It's sort of amazing what a difference it makes. I've stopped demanding the impossible. When things come up, I feel much calmer because I am thinking differently."

Reduce Past Event Triggers

Your Reacting Brain looks for, reacts to, and remembers threats, fear, and perceived dangers. This means that it remembers that you were scared but tends to forget that you survived and that fear was temporary.

Right or wrong, it easily learns that something *might be dangerous*; it does *not* easily learn that something is actually safe. That is not its job.

How does your Reacting Brain learn this? It notices what you feel, say, think, and do. And, it learns about dangers not only from your own *personal experiences*, it also learns about dangers from experiences you *hear about, see, or read*. It remembers and may react to *anything* it *associates* with fear, danger, or threat.

For example, if the shower scene in the movie "Psycho" frightened you, you may suddenly be afraid to take a shower in a hotel, or even at home. If you

Sidebar: Changing Unhelpful Self-Talk

Read the words in the first column and notice if they may make you feel stressed, tense, negative, or panicky. Now read the words in the second column and notice differences in feeling.

Each time you think or say a word or phrase in the first column, replace it with a word or phrase from the second column. Do this very deliberately. This may sound simplistic, but words are powerful, and you will be surprised by the effects of changing which words you choose.

Self-Talk Trigger	More Helpful Self-Talk
Should Ought Must Supposed to	I would prefer … It would be better if … I would like it if … Many people would …
Awful Terrible Horrible I can't stand it	Inconvenient Uncomfortable Unfortunate Unwanted
Never	Rarely Infrequently Hardly ever
Always	Often Most of the time Frequently Today
I can't	It is difficult to … I would be uncomfortable if … I won't I don't want to
What if?	So what?

were verbally or physically attacked, you may be frightened by anyone who looks or sounds like your attacker, or by being in a place similar to where you were attacked. If you were badly treated as a child, your Reacting Brain may jump in to help as if you were still that helpless child, forgetting that you are now an adult with power and choices.

Your Reacting Brain has learned lessons about whether you are vulnerable, or whether something is dangerous. The trouble is that many of those lessons are neither true nor helpful, or else they were true or helpful at some time in the past but no longer apply in the present.

Review your list of past event triggers on Form 3-06: Past Event List (page 59). What bad past events or experiences still trigger your Reacting Brain? What unhelpful lessons did your Reacting Brain learn from past events that cause it to misfire in the present?

Read This Caution First

If you have any traumatic past events such as being raped, molested, abused, assaulted, almost dying, seeing someone die, or being in a war, consult a mental health professional before using the technique described below on your own. Ask if this writing exercise is appropriate for you. Arrange for professional help if you think you may need it, or if you have signs of post-traumatic stress disorder (see Traumatic Stress on page 57).

Rethink Unhelpful Lessons and Reduce Past Event Triggers

You cannot change the past. However, you *can* change unhelpful lessons learned from these events and reduce the intensity of your emotional response to past event triggers.

What past experiences made you decide that panic was dangerous? Were there past events that made you feel helpless or vulnerable? Did things happen that made you feel that the world was chaotic or dangerous? That relaxing and letting down your guard was risky? Or that people are hurtful or unhelpful? Did someone or something teach you that you must be in control at all times?

Unhelpful lessons, like outdated maps, give bad directions. You need to update your Reacting Brain's maps about you, about panic, about your world, and about the people around you in your life now.

The writing technique below uses your Thinking Brain to help your Reacting Brain rethink unhelpful lessons from your past, learn helpful lessons that apply to you and your current reality, and decrease its emotional reaction.

Read all the instructions before you start writing. If you have several past event triggers, work on one event at a time. Think about any positive, helpful, or strengthening lessons you can learn, even from very bad or scary past events. Research shows that this type of writing helps people feel better, both physically and emotionally.

Relive

Write out the entire upsetting, past experience in the present tense as if you were living through it now. Because your Reacting Brain learns from experience, you want it to feel as if you were reliving the event. But you will know that you are safe, you have survived, and that you are revisiting this experience in order to lessen its impact, put it in perspective, and learn helpful lessons from it.

Include every detail from start to finish. Make it vivid. Write everything you saw, heard, felt, thought, said, or did. If you don't want to write, make a voice recording.

If reliving a past event makes you too anxious, complete the next two chapters first, then come back and try again. If it still makes you too anxious, finish the rest of the book before trying it. You can do this at your own pace. You are in charge of your own healing process. There is no deadline. Also consider whether talking with a therapist about the event might help you.

Rethink

The past is past. No matter how bad it was, or what you feared, or how badly you coped, you have survived. You are alive and you are working on making your life better.

Put into words any unhelpful lessons your Reacting Brain may have learned that could trigger anxiety in the present. Then reevaluate the event from the perspective of being older and wiser. Rethink what would be both true and helpful lessons to take from the experience.

What you would say to a friend, loved one, or someone you were mentoring or counseling who had this experience? Write that down. If you like, you can write this as if you were writing a letter to them. Say everything they need to hear. How would you want them to think about it? What are the most helpful lessons you would encourage them to take from it?

What positive lessons could you learn about your strengths, your resilience, or your coping skills? Was the experience or situation safer than you thought? Did any of the things you feared *not* actually happen? And if what you feared *did* happen, what lessons can you take from the experience that will be both *true and helpful?*

Are you wiser, stronger, or safer now than you were then? What can you learn from the experience that can be strengthening or life-affirming?

What positive lessons can you create from this experience? Do you have more empathy, wisdom, knowledge, or compassion as a result? Are you better able to help or comfort others, or advise them? Do you have a stronger awareness of—and gratitude for—good things in your life?

Write down all the lessons your Thinking Brain can draw from this event that will help your Reacting Brain in your present life.

Review Repeatedly

Reread what you have written or listen to the recording, imagining that it is happening. Relive it in your imagination because reliving activates your Reacting Brain so it is open to learning something new about the past.

Then read and review your new lessons, over and over again. Connecting the old event with new lessons helps change old pathways in your brain into new, more helpful ones. It takes time to groove a new pathway in the brain, so keep doing it.

With repetition, notice how you get less upset as you remember the past. The new lessons should begin to come to mind more and more easily, even when you are reliving the past event. (If this does not happen, consult a licensed mental health professional.)

Stories: Unhelpful Lessons from Past Events

Story: Amanda

As you may recall, Amanda's past events were repeated experiences of her alcoholic father being drunk, angry, and unpredictable. A more specific past event was being asleep in the car when he had an accident and she woke in terror. The unhelpful lessons her Reacting Brain learned from her childhood experiences were that she is vulnerable, that other people are unpredictable and can't be trusted or relied upon, that driving is dangerous, and that relaxing and sleeping is dangerous.

Amanda found it painful to write about her childhood, but she persevered because she realized her past was hurting her in the present. Writing helped her realize that her father could no longer put her in danger. She began to see herself as strong, resilient, and a good parent. She thought about the positive choices she has made to not be around people who mistreat her and began to be pleasant, but assertive, when her mother criticized her.

Then she wrote about the automobile accident. After reviewing what she wrote and rethinking it over and over, she noticed that not only was she feeling less tense while driving, she was finding it was easier to get to sleep at night.

Story: Raj

Raj's memory of food poisoning kept triggering anxiety and causing problems in the present. Because he *had* gotten physically sick after eating in public, his Reacting Brain decided that if he ever ate in public again he *would* get sick again.

This unhelpful lesson combined with another, much older unhelpful lesson. Throughout his childhood, Raj's parents stressed how important it was that he *never* embarrass or shame the family in any way. This lesson was taken so seriously that the idea of getting sick in public did not just feel embarrassing; it felt unbearable and unacceptable.

His Reacting Brain did not logically reason that Raj had never had food poisoning before or that it was very unlikely to happen again. Nor did his Reacting Brain consider that the other coworkers who got food poisoning from the buffet were not embarrassed and did not stop eating out. It also never questioned the messages he received from his parents.

Through doing the exercises in this book, Raj identified these unhelpful lessons and connected them to events in his past. He talked them over with his therapist and did the writing exercise described above for several different experiences.

After writing and rereading each of the writing exercises several times, he commented, "Not only am I starting to enjoy eating out again, I also realize that if something embarrassing does happen, it is not the end of the world. I can't tell you what a difference it makes to realize that." As a result, his personal and work relationships are better. He feels more relaxed about many things and is generally more comfortable, more confident, and less stressed.

Story: Liah

Liah's Reacting Brain learned several unhelpful lessons from her mother's hospitalization for depression. Because Liah thought it was her fault that her mother became depressed and left her, her Reacting Brain learned the lesson that Liah has to be perfect and make everyone happy or something bad will happen. Also, her Reacting Brain learned an unhelpful and untrue lesson that Liah would "go crazy" or "have a nervous breakdown".

On one level, Liah knew she had not caused her mother's depression. But it was only when she began writing about past events that she realized how firmly her child-like Reacting Brain had held onto a child's view of what had happened. After writing, rethinking, and reviewing, she told us, "I sort of knew it before, but now I really believe that it was not my fault. I was just a kid."

Writing about that past event made such a big difference that she spent several weeks writing, rethinking, and reviewing other past experiences such as times when she believed she had to be perfect and panic episodes when she thought she was going crazy. She said, "I feel so much better, like a weight has been lifted."

Story: Carlos

Carlos' past events were seeing his father and his grandfather have heart attacks. The unhelpful lesson his Reacting Brain learned from these two events was that Carlos was going to die of a heart attack, just like they did.

As Carlos wrote about these experiences, he thought more logically about the facts. His lifestyle and his health are very different from his father and grandfather's. They had multiple health problems that caused their heart attacks. Carlos, on the other hand, is in good health. His doctor has run many tests and his test results are all normal. He does not have the illnesses his relatives had, and he lives a much healthier life. After reliving, rethinking, and reviewing several times, Carlos reported, "I am not my father. I am not my grandfather. I have a strong heart and good health." His wife told us how much happier Carlos is.

This Week

Think about the anxiety triggers you have identified: genetic factors, chemicals, external stress, negative self-talk and/or unrealistic self-demands, and unhelpful lessons learned from past events. Decide what actions you will take to reduce *your* triggers.

You can spend a week–or more–focusing on reducing your triggers *before* moving on to the other steps of the program. Or you can work on reducing your triggers *while* reading and doing the steps described in the chapters ahead.

Keep filling out the Anxiety Record and the Panic Record forms. Look for useful information, patterns, insights and new lessons, for opportunities to use new skills and knowledge, and for signs of progress and change.

Form 9-99: Completed Chapter 9

Date completed: _____

Lessons learned:

_____

Chapter Summary

We have covered ways to reduce anxiety triggers including genetic, chemical, stress, self-talk, and past event triggers. You have also learned about important tools and strategies for managing stress, changing your self-talk, and thinking differently about past events.

Track your progress using Form 9-99: Completed Chapter 9. Note things you have learned, or been surprised by, in this chapter.

This completes Step 2. Check Form 1-03: Reward Plan (page 16) to see if you planned to reward yourself for completing this step.

Chapter 10

Step 3 Change Your Response to Sensations

"I felt anxiety, but I didn't let it take me over." – Angela

"I told myself it's just panic and panic is nothing to worry about."
— Robert

By now you know how the cycle of anxiety works and what triggers can activate it. You have learned about your *personal* anxiety cycle and may have started reducing your anxiety triggers. In steps 3-6, you break free from your personal anxiety cycle. This chapter teaches you to change your response to anxiety or panic sensations.

Continue to update your Form 8-02: Anxiety Record (page 110) every day and do a Form 8-03: Panic Record (page 114) every time you have even a brief surge of panic or anxiety – even if it is not a full panic attack. If you have not been using these forms, now is a good time to start. See Start Charting (page 108) to understand why these forms are important and how to use them.

Review the forms you have completed. What patterns do you see? What changes do you notice? What steps are you taking to reduce your anxiety triggers?

Practice Your ABCs: Accept, Breathe, Chart

Let's quickly recap what you have learned so far: Messages of threat trigger your poor, devoted—but dumb—caveman Reacting Brain into thinking you need to run away or fight. Its protective response to these messages is fast

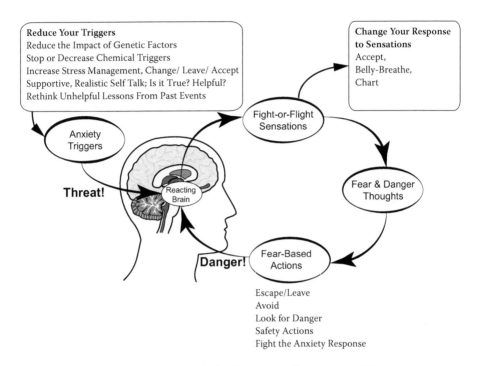

Figure 10-01: ABCs Accept, Breathe, Chart

and automatic. This response is hard-wired into you. Your body is designed to experience it. The fight-or-flight response helps you survive.

Based on this new understanding of what is happening, you will now change your reaction to fight-or-flight false alarms (panic attacks). Practice doing three things when this life-saving response misfires: *Accept, Belly Breathe,* and *Chart*. These are the ABCs of responding to a panic attack.

A - Accept

Remember what you learned about the anxiety cycle and the panic response. The more you accept a misfiring of your fight-or-flight system as unpleasant, uncomfortable, and a pain-in-the-neck nuisance—but *not* a life-threatening emergency—the more quickly it will pass and the less upsetting it will be. Remember that panic is both harmless and temporary.

The less you fight or fear the panic, the less your Reacting Brain will pump out adrenaline to "save you" from whatever it thinks you are fighting or fleeing.

Each surge of adrenaline *will* be used up. Your body *will* calm down. You can *safely wait out* the wave of panic. And there is a breathing technique that will help this process along: belly breathing.

B - Belly Breathing

In Chapter 2: The Anxiety Cycle you learned that the fight-or-flight response causes sympathetic nervous system arousal. Think "S" for "Save your life" or "Stress response."

The other branch of the nervous system is the parasympathetic nervous system. Think "P" for "Peaceful". Parasympathetic nervous system activation creates the opposite of the sympathetic nervous system's fight-or-flight response. It lowers your blood pressure, slows the heart rate, rebalances oxygen and carbon dioxide, relaxes muscles, reduces tension, and so on.

Good News

You can activate the peaceful branch of your nervous system simply by changing your breathing. You can minimize the unpleasant effects of unneeded sympathetic arousal by switching to slow diaphragmatic breathing, or "belly breathing."

We are born breathing this way naturally. If you watch a baby breathing as it lies on its back, the baby's belly rises with each breath it takes in (inhales); and falls as the breath goes out (exhales).

Discover for yourself the difference between two ways of breathing: chest breathing and diaphragmatic belly breathing.

Do It Now – Chest Breathing

Put one hand on your chest and the other hand over your belly button. Now in a minute–not yet—do two things: 1) take a big chest breath and hold it and 2) notice which hand moved and notice all the tension in your body.

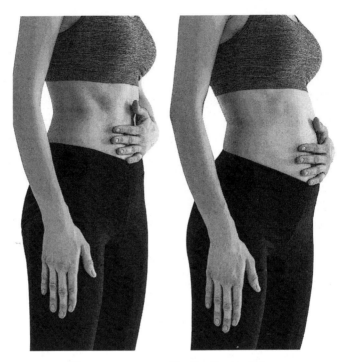

Figure 10-02: Belly Breathing

Ready? Go ahead. Take a big <u>chest</u> breath. Hold it, and notice that your *upper* hand moved. Notice the feelings of tension in your chest, neck, and shoulders.

Okay. Let it out and relax. This is how you do NOT want to breathe. We call this chest breathing.

Lots of people, when they are told to "take a deep breath", take a big chest breath. This increases muscle tension and can easily cause hyperventilating (overbreathing) which can create anxiety sensations. For more detail on hyperventilating, see Chapter 5: Your Anxiety or Panic Sensations.

Do It Now – Belly Breathing: Low and Slow

With chest breathing, the upper hand moves and the lower hand on your stomach stays still. When you breathe using your diaphragm, the upper hand stays still and the lower hand on your stomach moves in and out. You want to breathe using your diaphragm.

The diaphragm is a thin layer of muscle located below your lungs, between the chest and abdomen. It helps you breathe. When you breathe in using your diaphragm, it moves down and pushes your stomach out. That is why another name for this is "belly breathing". This breathing may be familiar to you from yoga, meditation, relaxation, singing, or competitive sports.

Think low and slow. You want your breathing to be *low* in the belly, and to be *slow* and rhythmic. *The exhale* (when you release the breath and breathe out) *should be especially slow.*

I like to count silently from one to four with each breath in, and from one to four with each breath out. Some people count to different numbers, or silently say 'relax' as they breathe out.

The thing to remember is that you want your breathing to be:

• LOW (in the belly) and

• SLOW and rhythmic

Put one hand on your chest and the other on your stomach. Ready?

Now, breathe in so the air pushes your lower hand out and your upper hand barely moves at all. Count silently from one to four as you breathe in, and more slowly from one to four as you slowly breathe out. Feel the rhythm.

One, two, three, four as you breathe in. One, two, three, four as you breathe out. Slow and smooth.

Breathe deep into the belly: Low and Slow. As you slowly exhale, you may notice a wave of relaxation moving from your head and neck into your shoulders, down your arms, into your back, and through your body. Let your muscles settle and relax. Feel yourself become calmer and more grounded.

Continue for up to four minutes.

What did you notice?

Most people feel calmer, less tense or worried, more relaxed, or more peaceful. Some people even yawn and feel sleepy. What did *you* notice?

If belly breathing came easily to you, congratulations. If you had trouble breathing this way, or felt like you were not getting enough air, read on.

Other ways to learn and practice this breathing

Virtual Reality (VR)

Some virtual reality systems designed for use in psychotherapy include teaching materials for diaphragmatic belly breathing. If you are working with a therapist who has a suitable VR program, ask about trying this learning experience. In virtual reality, you can be transported into relaxing virtual environments that can help you to slow your breathing and relax your muscles.

You may also be able to record the instructions on your phone and listen to them when you practice belly breathing at home.

Relaxation Apps

You may be interested in using an app to help you learn and practice belly breathing. I recommend the Breathe2Relax app to my clients for a number of reasons. It is free and can be used on either an iPhone or Android phone. It was developed by the Veterans' Administration with input from psychologists and has been research-tested for effectiveness. You can choose the length of the in-breath and the out-breath. It also has options for soothing images and recorded instructions.

Hundreds of other apps are available. You may find an app that helps you learn and practice belly breathing. However, be somewhat cautious in believing the marketing claims for apps. Many apps are neither developed by mental health professionals nor researched to evaluate their actual effectiveness. I would encourage you to make sure that any app you use is consistent with what you are learning here.

If you have trouble shifting your breathing

If you have trouble shifting your breathing, try these two approaches:

1. Squeeze your stomach muscles to push all the air out as you exhale. Relax them as you breathe air in again.

2. Practice at first lying down on your back. Put a small book on your chest and another on your stomach and lightly place a hand on each book. When you breathe in, feel the incoming breath lift the book on

your stomach. When you breathe out, feel the book lower back down. Count from one to four with each breath in and out. After you can do belly breathing lying down, practice without the books while sitting and standing.

If you struggle with belly breathing or feel like there is a fight between the body wanting to breathe high in the chest and you trying to move the breath to the belly, this can be a sign that you are chronically tense. Think about your triggers. Your Reacting Brain may want to keep you on 'partial red alert' ready to respond to danger at any moment. Identifying and reducing your anxiety triggers and practicing belly breathing may be very helpful.

Did you feel like you did not get enough air?

This is often a sign that you have been chronically hyperventilating—which actually means that belly breathing will be particularly helpful for you. You just need to practice.

Begin by practicing for only 30-60 seconds. Add in short practices throughout the day. Gradually extend your practice time until you can belly breathe comfortably for up to four minutes.

Practicing: The Four 4s

There are many ways to learn and practice diaphragmatic breathing. The main thing is for your breathing to be low (in the belly) and slow.

One easy-to-remember way is **Four 4s**:

- Practice **4** times a day
- **4** minutes at a time
- Count from 1 to **4** with each breath in
- Count from 1 to **4** with each breath out

Four 4s: **4** times a day, **4** minutes at a time, **4** counts in, **4** counts out.

I don't have time to practice!

Four 4-minute sessions are best, but if the only time you can practice is in bed at night and in the bathroom during the day, do it then. Do short practices when you sit down to eat, every time you stop in traffic, every time you pick up the phone. Start practicing whenever you think about it during the day. Even changing for one or two breaths can be helpful.

Why practice?

Like every skill, the more you practice, the better you get. The better you get, the better it feels, and the easier it becomes to shift into this breathing.

Begin first with scheduled practices. Then use this breathing any time you notice tension. Next, start low and slow breathing *before* doing anything that may make you anxious.

Finally, use low and slow belly breathing during panic attacks. It helps you accept and tolerate the unpleasantness of unnecessary panic and helps the sensations be milder and end sooner. Count as described in the instructions to avoid breathing too quickly (hyperventilating).

Avoid This Trap

You can actually make your anxiety worse over time if you use belly breathing in a desperate, frightened attempt to fight the anxiety response and make it stop because you are terrified something bad will happen if you are unable to stop or lessen the sensations.

This makes sense when you look at the anxiety cycle. Belly breathing for this purpose is a panic action and is motivated by fear. You are doing belly breathing as a way of *fighting* the anxiety response. You are breathing because your panic thoughts *fear* something bad will happen if you don't stop the sensations. Fighting panic out of fear *strengthens* the anxiety cycle, rather than weakening it.

If you *tell* yourself panic is not dangerous, but *act* as if it is, your Reacting Brain will believe your *actions*. Use belly breathing to help you tolerate the unpleasant sensations of a misfired fight-or-flight response, while accepting that misfires and false alarms happen and are unneeded, unpleasant, temporary, and harmless. Do *not* use belly breathing in a terrified attempt to fight or escape the natural, life-saving—but misguided—panic sensations.

I sometimes demonstrate this in therapy by asking, "What would you think if I suddenly jumped up, locked the door, leaned against the door with all my weight, and shouted, 'Don't worry! Nothing's wrong! There is no danger!

Figure 10-03: There's nothing wrong!

We will now all climb out the window because it's good exercise!' Would you believe my words—or my actions?"

Right.

Actions *always* speak louder than words!

C – Chart

Panic and anxiety records help you learn your anxiety cycle and track your progress as you make changes and break the cycle.

Panic Record

With Panic Records, you analyze and learn from each episode of panic or anxiety. The more you analyze what happened, the better you know what you want to change.

Every time you have a surge of anxiety, complete a Panic Record. Even if it is not a full panic attack, complete a form anyway. The more you know about your triggers, sensations, scary panic thoughts, and fear-motivated actions, the more powerful and effective you will be at breaking your anxiety cycle.

If you have been filling out Panic Records, great! Keep up the good work.

If you have not been using these forms, start now. See Panic Record (page 109) for panic record instructions and examples. My experience shows that people who use the forms get the fastest and most long-lasting results.

Anxiety Record

Anxiety Records track your progress day-by-day and week-by-week. Fill out this form every night and summarize at the end of each week.

If you are already filling out Anxiety Records, terrific! If you have not been using this form, give it a try. It takes only a few seconds and is encouraging to see progress and patterns. See Anxiety Record (page 108).

This Week

Start practicing your ABC's (Accepting, Belly breathing, and Charting). Continue noticing your anxiety triggers and working to reduce them.

Fill out Anxiety and Panic Record forms. Look for patterns. Look for changes. Look for progress. Notice how your experience fits the anxiety cycle. Where can you weaken and break this cycle?

You can spend a week on these activities or you can move ahead to the next chapter. There is no deadline. Take as much time as you need to understand and begin using the skills you are learning.

Chapter Summary

In this chapter you have learned to change how you respond to panic symptoms including specific techniques for acceptance and belly breathing. We have also reviewed the importance of charting with Panic Records.

Track your progress using Form 10-99: Completed Chapter 10. Note things you have learned, or been surprised by, in this chapter.

Form 10-99: Completed Chapter 10

Date completed:
_____

Lessons learned:

_____

This completes Step 3. Check Form 1-03: Reward Plan (page 16) to see how you planned to reward yourself for completing this step.

Chapter 11

Step 4 Change Your Thinking

"When the panic and anxiety started, it was like a door opened in my mind and all this fear kept pouring through. I tried for years to get that door to shut again, but it wouldn't stay shut! Now I know it's okay for it to be open because I don't have to be afraid of what's coming in through the door." – Lisa

I hope that by now you have been practicing your ABCs: Accepting anxiety or panic sensations, Belly breathing, and Charting. What are you noticing?

Review your recent Form 8-02: Anxiety Records (page 110) and Form 8-03: Panic Records (page 114). What patterns do you see? Have there been changes in the number of panic attacks (or spurts of anxiety), your overall anxiety level, or your worry about panic?

What changes are you seeing in your Panic Records? What changes have you made to break your anxiety cycle? What changes are you considering making?

In this chapter, you will learn to change your response to fear and danger thoughts related to panic. Help your Thinking Brain evaluate what your Reacting Brain is shouting. Figure out when a panic response is sending at true alarm and when it is sending a false alarm.

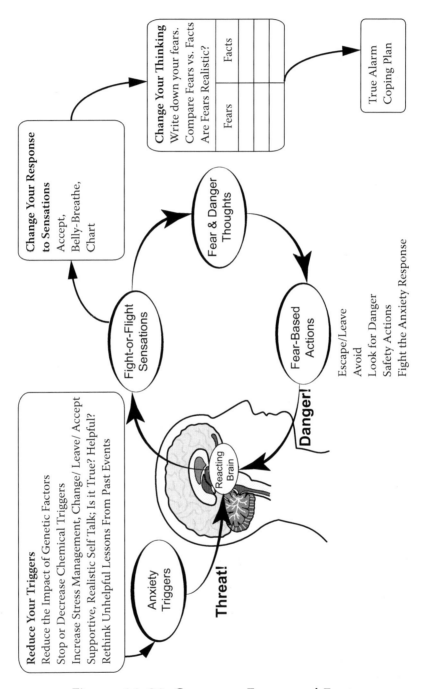

Figure 11-01: Compare Fears and Facts

True Alarm or False Alarm?

When your primitive, protective Reacting Brain alerts you and instantly responds to *an actual threat*, it is sending what we call a "true alarm". There *is* real danger. True alarms are reality-based and lifesaving.

Unfortunately, the Reacting Brain, as you know, can also send "false alarms" activating the fight-or-flight response *in the absence of danger*.

How do you decide whether the reaction you are experiencing is a true alarm or a false alarm? This is an important question.

Let's start with an example from the movies. In westerns, sometimes the hero's horse suddenly becomes skittish, alerting the hero to an unseen danger. Like the Reacting Brain, horses sometimes sense a danger the rider doesn't see, like a snake in the grass or an enemy hidden in the trees; but, like your Reacting Brain, horses can also be spooked by things that are completely harmless.

In the movies, when his horse gets jittery, sometimes the hero will look around, see the danger, and gallop off to safety, dodging bullets all the way: "That was an ambush! You saved my life, boy!"

But sometimes the hero looks around and reassures the horse, overriding its reaction: "Steady, boy. That's just my girlfriend riding up for a love scene."

It's pretty important to know when there's real danger, and when it's a false alarm. You don't want to get ambushed, but you don't want to miss the love scene either!

In some ways, your Reacting Brain is the horse and you are the rider. You don't want to ignore a *true* alarm. You just don't want to trust a *false* alarm.

How do you tell the difference? You change from reacting to thinking, from using your Reacting Brain to using your Thinking Brain. When your Reacting Brain fires an alarm, you activate your Thinking Brain.

First, you figure out what danger your Reacting Brain thinks is threatening you. Then you get the facts you need to decide whether the danger really exists. The facts help your Thinking Brain decide whether this danger is real, and your Reacting Brain should be listened to, or whether this is a false alarm and your Reacting Brain should be reassured and ignored.

There are three skills in this step:

1. Put fears into words

2. Get the facts

3. Compare the fears with the facts and decide if your Reacting Brain is sending a true alarm or a false alarm

Put Fears into Words - Listen to the Reacting Brain

To reassure your Reacting Brain, you must figure out what is worrying it. What *dangers* does it think are threatening you? What is it *assuming*? What is it *predicting*? You need to know what it fears, so you can get the relevant facts.

Take this example. Your Reacting Brain fears that panic means you are going crazy. Getting proof that you are not having a heart attack doesn't help because that information is not relevant. Those facts do not address the fear. You need facts about whether or not you are going crazy.

And vice versa. If your Reacting Brain fears you are having a heart attack, facts that you are not going crazy are pretty useless. You need facts about your *physical* health, not your *mental* health. Knowing what your Reacting Brain fears is happening (or might happen) lets you know what facts your Thinking Brain needs.

You have to find out what threats your Reacting Brain thinks you face before you can decide whether or not you are in danger; whether the panic is a "true" alarm or a "false" alarm. Review your Form 6-01: Fear and Danger Thoughts Checklist (page 89) and your recent Form 8-03: Panic Records (page 114). Which fears did you check off or add to the list?

Most people try *not* to think about their fears. I am asking you *to think* about them. Think really hard about what you fear may happen. Put your worst nightmare fears into words. Imagine your most feared outcome and write it down. Get very specific. Spell it out.

IF what was happening was dangerous, what might the danger be? And if *that* were true, then what? And if *that* were true, then what? And so on.

Ask your Reacting Brain to tell you (or show you in images) what it fears might happen. What might go wrong? What would that mean? What are the worst possible outcomes?

Your Thinking Brain needs to act like a loving parent to your child-like Reacting Brain. If a child is convinced there are monsters in the bedroom, you don't just say "Oh, shut up."

You ask where the child thinks the monsters are because only by knowing where exactly the monsters are hiding can you prove that there *are no monsters* there. Showing that there is no monster in the closet does not reassure a child who thinks there's a monster hiding under the bed.

What does your (remember, devoted but *dumb*, well-intentioned but *misinformed*) child-like bodyguard Reacting Brain fear? What "dangers" is it "protecting" you from?

Put all your fears and worries into words. This helps you use your Thinking Brain to decide whether your panic is in response to a true alarm or a false alarm.

"My fear thoughts are questions"

Sometimes fear thoughts are phrased as questions. Here are some examples: "What if everyone sees I'm anxious?" "What if I feel short of breath and scared?" "What if I panic while I'm driving, or eating, or alone, or with other people?"

So, let's talk about questions. A question is only scary when we fear the answer, or when there is an unspoken—but scary—assumption underlying the question.

For example, imagine that you are back in school and think "What if there's a test today?" Depending on what you think the answer to that question is, you may feel scared and panicked, or excited and pleased.

If your answer to the question "What if there's a test today?" is "What if I didn't study enough? I bet I didn't. Oh no! I'll probably fail!" The question was really shorthand for "A test would be dangerous because I will fail it." You will be likely have a panic attack.

But imagine your answer to the question "What if there's a test today?" is "Awesome. I have studied. I understand this material. I bet I'll ace it. No problem. I can totally do this. Bring it on." You will be excited and pleased.

See how the question is either scary, or not, depending on what you think the answer is? When your fear thought is a question, answer the question.

Sometimes exploring possible answers to a question uncovers assumptions or predictions. Exploring your answer to "what if there's a test?" might uncover assumptions like "I shouldn't even bother studying because I'm stupid just like my foster parents said." or predictions like "I just know I'll flunk the test. My GPA will drop. I will probably have to drop out, so I'll never graduate, never get a job, and be a failure."

Same question thought. Different answers, different assumptions, different prediction, and *very* different reactions.

If questions come to your mind that scare you (like "what if I panic?!?"), uncover and put into words what you (or your Reacting Brain) fear might be the answer.

If the answer to the question, "What if everyone sees I'm having a panic attack?" is "They will think I'm weird, crazy, and incompetent. I will be fired, I will never get another job, and I will end up homeless and alone!", then the question will frighten you and you will fear panic.

On the other hand, if the answer to the question, "What if everyone sees I'm having a panic attack?" is "So what? Anxiety is a human emotion and no big deal. One out of every three people had a panic attack in the last year. Most people are really sympathetic when they see someone is nervous." then your panic will be an uncomfortable annoyance, but not frightening.

When your fear thought is a question, write down all the possible scary answers, assumptions, or feared outcomes. Those are your fears.

"I don't know my fears"

If you can't put your fears into words or can't identify specific fears, reread your Form 6-01: Fear and Danger Thoughts Checklist (page 89). Think about each fear or possible danger. Think about those times when you feel (or have felt) panicky, afraid, or anxious. Check off any fears on the list you have experienced and add other fears that come to your mind.

Review your Form 8-03: Panic Records (page 114) and ask yourself "What would be the worst thing if that *did* happen, or if my fear thoughts *were* true? What would that mean for me or my future?" Keep digging deeper and deeper repeatedly asking questions such as "What would that mean? What would be bad about that? And then what would happen? And then what? And what if that did happen?" Keep going until you can identify your very worst nightmare scenarios.

If someone else was in a situation similar to yours, and the physical sensations or the situation scared them, what fears or thoughts do you think they might be having? What might they be worried about?

If you continue to have trouble identifying your fears, trying using a Scheduled Daily Worry Time (see page 165). Worry time can help you translate your Reacting Brain's worries and fears into words, so your Thinking Brain can take over.

Story: Carlos

Carlos knew exactly what he feared. He was afraid that his body sensations meant that he was having a heart attack. He feared he would die like his father and grandfather. He worried that his death would leave his family struggling financially. "What if my wife can't make the payments and loses the house? What if she can't care for the grandchildren and my kids lose their jobs? What if I die before everyone is provided for? What will happen to them?" He feared death and he worried about the burden his death would place on his family.

Story: Liah

Liah had trouble identifying her fears. She knew she put a lot of pressure on herself (self-demands triggers), was drinking too much caffeine (chemical triggers), and was influenced by her mother's history of depression and anxiety (genetic factors and past event triggers). However, there was more to her anxiety cycle than just triggers.

Her therapist asked questions that helped Liah explore what her Reacting Brain was afraid might happen.

Question: "What is it that your Reacting Brain fears? What would be the worst-case scenario?"

Liah: "I don't know…Maybe it's afraid that I might not do a good job at work."

Question: "And if you didn't do a good job, what would that mean?"

Liah: "Well, that would mean that I'm not as competent as other people think I am."

Question: "And if you weren't that competent, then what would that mean? What would be the worst thing about that or what would that mean about you or your future?"

Liah: "They would think I was a fraud and a liar. I could be fired."

Question: "And what if you got fired? Then what?"

Liah: "That would be awful! What would I do with my life then?"

Question: "What is the scary answer to that question?"

Liah: "I would have no job and I would hate myself for messing up so bad."

Question: "What would it mean about you if you messed up and lost your job or made a big mistake?"

Liah (starting to tear up): "It would mean that I let myself down. If I made a big mistake, like losing my job, it would mean I was losing control."

Question: "And what would it mean if you lost control? What would be the worst thing about that?"

Liah: "It would mean I was having a breakdown! And, what if I never recovered? That is my worst nightmare fear, that I could end up like my mother."

By looking deeply into what her Reacting Brain might be predicting, Liah identified her worst fears: the fear of losing control of herself and "going crazy" like her mother. Having figured out what her caveman Reacting Brain feared, she could use her Thinking Brain to evaluate and challenge those fears.

"I worry about a lot of things"

"My life has been filled with terrible misfortunes, most of which never happened." – Mark Twain

If you worry a lot, or if you worry about many different things, schedule a daily time during which you write down all your worries. Scheduled Daily Worry Time sounds like a crazy suggestion, but it can actually reduce worrying. It can also help you identify what is worrying your Reacting Brain.

You may have noticed that when you try to push worries away because they make you anxious, they tend to come back and be even stronger. It is as if your Reacting Brain keeps nagging, trying to get your attention. When you push it away, it worries you haven't heard its warning and nags louder and longer, or more often.

You *do* need to listen and put your worries into words. You do *not* want to worry all the time. Scheduled Daily Worry Time helps you uncover fears and gives relief from worrying during the rest of the day.

Schedule a Worry Time

Every day, schedule 15 to 30 minutes of worry time. During this time, do nothing but worry. Don't be rational. Don't plan. Don't evaluate or challenge your worries. Just worry.

Write down all the worries you can remember or think of, big or little. Coax your Reacting Brain to tell you everything that it fears may happen.

If you need it, use a timer to signal the end of your worry time. When worry time is up, get busy. Actively do other things until tomorrow's worry time.

When worries come to mind during *other times*, pause, make a note of the worry, promise to think about it during your next scheduled worry time, and go back to what you were doing. Be sure to keep your promise and write about that worry during your next scheduled worry time.

If you cannot sleep because you are worrying, get out of bed and write down every worry. Then reassure your Reacting Brain that you have listened and now it is safe for you to go to sleep.

Engage the Thinking Brain: Get the Facts

*"It isn't what we don't know that gives us trouble;
it's what we know that ain't so."*
— Will Rogers

Once you know what your Reacting Brain is afraid of, have your Thinking Brain analyze, question, evaluate, and challenge those fears. Your Thinking Brain needs facts to convince it to override your Reacting Brain.

The fight-or-flight response is a healthy, intense, harmless, life-saving physical response designed to save your life by preparing you to run or fight. Since this response is triggered by the Reacting Brain, it can go off when there is no danger, *but* it is always trying to protect you even if it misfires when you don't need or want it.

Since panic attacks can be scary, we will first review important facts about the physical sensations of panic. Then we will quickly review some key facts about panic and anxiety in general.

Facts about Anxiety or Panic Sensations

Here is a quick summary of the purpose behind each anxiety or panic sensation. For more detailed information, review chapters 2 The Anxiety Cycle, 3 Your Personal Anxiety Cycle, and 5 Your Anxiety or Panic Sensations.

Physical Sensations	Cause or Protective Purpose
Palpitations (stronger, faster heartbeats)	Heart is pumping more blood to the fighting muscles to help you fight or run
Faster breathing	Sends more oxygen to fuel the muscles
Muscle tension, chest tightness or discomfort	Muscles are tensed, preparing to fight or run

Physical Sensations	Cause or Protective Purpose
Short of breath or suffocating feeling	Faster breathing sends extra oxygen to muscles, but you're not running or fighting, so the oxygen/ carbon dioxide balance is off
Feeling hot	Blood is sent to the fighting muscles
Feeling cold, tingling, or numbness	Caused by overbreathing and by blood vessels constricting to reduce bleeding if you get wounded
Visual changes	Pupils dilate to increase your range of vision so you won't be ambushed
Feeling faint, dizzy, or unsteady	Caused by changes in blood flow, overbreathing, and dilated pupils
Feeling like things aren't quite real or like you're not quite real	Caused by visual changes and decreased concentration on everyday activities while focusing on potential dangers
Stomach discomfort, nausea, or diarrhea	Digestion slows down because blood is moved to the fighting muscles
Lump in throat, dry throat, or feeling like you can't swallow	Muscles are tense and salivation slows; you're not going to eat if you're in danger
Shaky, trembling	Muscles are tensed but not being used
Sweating	So you won't overheat if you run or fight
Easily startled, restless, feeling you're going to "do something"	You're being prepared to respond to danger

Physical Sensations	Cause or Protective Purpose
More easily irritated	You're being prepared to fight off danger
Insomnia or restless sleep	You're alert for danger
Decreased concentration	Your mind's thinking about danger

Facts About Panic and Anxiety

Here are some common fears about panic and the incredibly reassuring facts. For more detailed information, review chapters 2 The Anxiety Cycle, 3 Your Personal Anxiety Cycle, and 6 Your Fear and Danger Thoughts.

Fears	Facts
If you are panicky or anxious it means you are in danger.	Not necessarily. Panic or anxiety can be triggered without real danger.
Panic sensations mean something is physically wrong.	No. Panic sensations only mean your fight-or-flight response was triggered.
Panic will always get worse and worse over time and will happen more and more often no matter what.	No. Your actions and responses to panic make the difference. What you think and do strengthens the anxiety cycle, or weakens it.
A panic attack could continue forever and never stop.	A panic attack cannot continue forever. You run out of adrenaline and your body activates the peaceful side of the nervous system. You can't panic forever. If you are chronically worried and tense, learn and practice anxiety and stress reduction skills.

Fears	Facts
Panic can make people go crazy.	Panic cannot make you go crazy. Crazy and panic are two separate conditions.
People will know when I have a panic attack. They will think I'm weak, incompetent, or crazy.	Most people, even in panic treatment groups, cannot tell when others are panicking. People who know another person is anxious are usually sympathetic and want to help.
Panic will make me completely nonfunctional, incoherent, and/or paralyzed.	Panic is life-saving and helps you fight or run. Being paralyzed, incoherent, or nonfunctional doesn't help you run or fight. A response that did that wouldn't be passed on.
I'll go out of control or do something crazy.	You may feel revved up because you are prepared to fight or flee, but panic doesn't make you go out of control or crazy.
Feeling faint or dizzy means I'm likely to pass out.	You are being prepared to run or fight, not pass out. The changes in breathing, vision, and blood flow make you feel dizzy but are the opposite of what has to happen for you to faint.
Anxiety can make me stop breathing, suffocate, choke to death, or be unable to swallow.	You may feel this way because of tense muscles, breathing changes, and a dry mouth. You won't suffocate or die. That's not life-saving.

Fears	Facts
Panic will damage my body. It is causing physical harm.	This natural life-saving response is designed to protect you. It is *chronic tension* that can cause health problems. Check with your healthcare provider if you have high blood pressure or a past heart attack.

Compare Fears vs. Facts

This is where you activate your Thinking Brain to compare your fears against the facts.

After identifying specific fears that alarm your Reacting Brain, use your Thinking Brain to evaluate whether those fears are correct. You can help your Thinking Brain do this by finding appropriate *facts*, comparing fears to facts, and putting things *in perspective*.

This is essential because you take completely different actions depending on whether your Reacting Brain is sending a true alarm or a false alarm:

In a true alarm: the *facts agree with the fears*. You have *a real-life problem* and need a plan to cope with the problem. The Reacting Brain is serving its purpose by alerting you to a real threat. Your Thinking Brain can now plan how to avoid or cope with the threat.

In a false alarm: the *facts disagree with the fears*. You have an *anxiety problem*. You need to take action based on the *facts*, not your fear. Your Reacting Brain has misunderstood the situation. Your Thinking Brain needs to take over.

In this step, you focus on the facts—not your feelings, not your body's reaction, not the thoughts that pop into your brain when you are scared—just the facts. Turn things over to your smart, rational Thinking Brain.

Create your personal Fears vs. Facts table to compare your fears against the facts. This table is a way to get your Reacting Brain and your Thinking Brain to talk with one another.

Record your fears and facts using Form 11-01: Fears vs. Facts (page 172) or by creating a similar table using your computer.

Your Fears

In the "Fears" column, write down every fearful, upsetting thought you can uncover, deduce, guess, or imagine might be worrying your Reacting Brain. Every time your fearful, protective caveman Reacting Brain comes up with another "But what if....?" type of thought, add that thought in a new row.

Put only one fear per row. Use as many rows as you need. If more fears come to mind, add more rows. Your records can help you identify your fears and put them into words.

Try stating your fears in "If…, then…" form. For example, "If I have a panic attack, then I will pass out." "If my chest is tight and I feel short of breath, then I am suffocating and will die if I don't get fresh air."

It often helps to write a fear as if it is universally true, in other words that it is true every time and for every person. For example, "Every time I have panicked, I have passed out." or "Every time the panic reaction is triggered, the person suffocates and dies unless they get fresh air. Panic kills unless there is fresh air."

Writing fears in this way helps your Thinking Brain identify the holes in logic and can highlight how fears are not actually true. Rather than reacting emotionally, you start thinking logically: "Wait a minute! I haven't passed out every time I had a panic attack. That's not true." or "I know that everyone who panics doesn't suffocate and die if they're not outside. That's ridiculous."

Review your Form 8-03: Panic Records (page 114). Write thoughts that still scare you in the Fears column. Go over your Panic Records to look for any sensations, situations, or actions that still scare you. Explore what frightens you about these and add those thoughts in the fears column.

Reread your ratings on Form 5-01: Anxiety or Panic Sensations (page 73). If any of these sensations still scare you, think about why they scare you. What are you afraid is happening? What is your Reacting Brain assuming or predicting? Add those fear thoughts.

Go back over your Form 6-01: Fear and Danger Thoughts Checklist (page 89). Make sure that each fear you checked off is included in the fears column.

Form 11-01: Fears vs. Facts

Fears	Facts	Realistic?

Reread your Form 7-01: Fear-Based Actions Checklist (page 96). Think about the fears, the predictions, or the assumptions that are behind your fear-based actions. Why do you take each fear-based action? What do you fear will happen if you don't take that action? Add any fears that are not covered already.

Review your lists of negative self-talk on Form 3-04: Negative Self-Talk Checklist (page 51) and unrealistic self-demands on Form 3-05: Unrealistic Self-Demands Checklist (page 52). Look at your past events list on Form 3-06: Past Events List (page 59) and consider the unhelpful lessons your Reacting Brain may have learned. Add all these to the fears column. Add any thoughts that might trigger a false alarm.

If some new fear or worry thought comes up during your Scheduled Daily Worry Time, add it to the fears column.

The Facts

The right column is the "Facts" column. In this column, you use your Thinking Brain to evaluate how likely or how true each fear thought is.

Write down all the facts and evidence. Ask questions like "Is each statement in the left column literally true?" "Does what it predicts really happen?", then write the answers in the facts column. Add the facts about panic and the anxiety cycle.

If, like Carlos, you have fears about your health, include the results of relevant medical tests or exams. Write what other people have told you, IF they are reliable, knowledgeable, and objective. For more facts about your health, ask your healthcare provider. If you look for information online, go to *reliable* sources like government websites or reputable professional organizations. Avoid websites trying to sell you something or making incredible claims and be very skeptical of anything posted by people you do not know and who do not know you.

Be logical. Look for holes in the evidence or logic behind thoughts that trigger panic. Articulate and challenge the underlying assumptions. Put things in perspective.

Use everything you have learned so far. Explain why the fear thought is either justified and helpful, or *not*. And whenever the statement in the left column is either *not* entirely true or *not* helpful, write what *is* true and what *would be* more helpful. Write what you would tell someone else.

Help your Thinking Brain analyze, consider, question, and challenge each thought in the left column. One by one, match them against the facts and put them in perspective.

Questions can help uncover important relevant facts. You will read below how Amanda used questions to complete her Fears vs. Facts table.

Question Your Fears to Uncover Facts

Ask yourself questions such as:

- What are the facts? What evidence do I have that my fears are true – or not true?

- How often has my worst fear *actually happened* compared to how many times I *thought it might* happen?

- How bad is this *really*? If the "awful" thing actually happened, how bad would that really be? How would I cope? How long would it last?

- How does this compare to real catastrophes like war, natural disasters, etc.? Would what I fear be truly terrible, or would it be unpleasant, difficult, embarrassing, or painful, but not "horrible" or "unbearable"?

- What are more helpful ways to think about this that are still realistic?

Asking questions and finding answers helps you change panic-provoking thinking to helpful thinking grounded in facts and evidence, logical reasoning, realistic expectations, and coping strategies. Make your answers specific, factual, and detailed.

Ask, "What is the worst? What are the facts? How likely is this *really*? Is this 100% guaranteed to be true? How often have I had this fear, worry, or sensation? How often has what I feared or predicted *actually happened*?"

Your Reacting Brain can be very prone to common unhelpful ways of thinking such as jumping to false conclusions, predicting something bad will happen, or catastrophizing and blowing things out of proportion.

Story: Amanda

Here are some examples of how Amanda's Reacting Brain jumped to false conclusions, predicted bad things would happen, and catastrophized. These are labeled in the examples below to help you identify them. Amanda used questions to help her Thinking Brain come up with truer, more helpful thinking.

Predicting: "If I go to the mall, I'll have a panic attack for sure."

Questions: "What are the facts? How likely is this *really*?"

Answers: "I can't predict whether I'll have a panic attack or not. Maybe I won't have a panic attack. I've been to the mall hundreds of times in my life, and only had a panic attack at the mall one time. It's pretty unlikely that I would panic."

Catastrophizing: "Yes but what if I did! That would be horrible!"

Questions: "What if I do panic? So what? How bad is that *really*? How would I cope?"

Answers: "Well, even if I did have a panic attack, I guess it wouldn't be so bad. Panic attacks are uncomfortable, and I wouldn't like it, but I could tolerate the symptoms. I could use the breathing skills and remind myself that this is temporary. And, even when I have had a panic attack in the past, I have always survived them."

Jumping to a false conclusion and predicting: "When I have a panic attack, I can't breathe. I'll suffocate. Feeling dizzy and short of breath proves that."

Questions: "What are the facts? How likely is this *really*?"

Answers: "First of all, I am predicting the future. I don't know what is going to happen; I certainly don't know for sure that I would suffocate. Let's look at the facts. I've never suffocated during past panic attacks. I don't have asthma. My lungs work. The point of panic is to help you run or fight, so you wouldn't suffocate. My throat doesn't close up even though it feels like it does. Feeling like you aren't getting enough air is common with panic. The fact is you breathe more oxygen than you need during a panic attack, so I'm actually breathing more than normal, not less. I am not going to suffocate."

Questions: "How bad is this feeling *really*? How could I cope if I felt like I was suffocating?"

Answers: "Even if I did have the feeling of not getting enough air, I could remind myself of the facts. I could write down the facts about panic attacks on a piece of paper or on my phone to have with me at the mall. That way, I could pull it out to remind myself of the facts if I get anxious while I'm there. That would help. Plus, I can practice my belly breathing."

False conclusion, predicting, catastrophizing: "Panic feels dangerous so it must <u>be</u> dangerous. If I don't have my anxiety pills with me at all times, I will definitely have a panic attack. That would be unbearable!"

Questions: "What are the facts? Is this really true? How likely is this *really*? Even if it happened, how bad would it be *really*? How would I cope?"

Answers: "Having the pills with me is a "safety action" and makes me more likely to have panic again even though it helps in the moment. Just carrying the pills does not actually prevent panic. Panic is caused by my triggers and what I say and do. Actually, I've forgotten my pills before and I was just fine. I suppose it wouldn't be unbearable, I could handle it."

Story: Liah

Liah recorded her fears and challenged them with facts, as shown in the example below (see page 178).

Using Numbers to Uncover Facts

You can also use numbers to evaluate fears. Liah found this approach particularly useful and convincing. This is how you use numbers:

1. Write down the actual number of times you have worried about something or had anxiety or panic sensations.

2. Then write down the actual number of times what you worried about or feared actually occurred.

3. Compare the numbers.

Story: Liah

Liah used numbers as well as questions to compare her fears to the facts. Here is the example she shared with her treatment group.

"I started the job 9 months ago and I panic every Monday morning on my way to work." Since this has happened for 9 months and there are 4 weeks in most months, Liah multiplied 4 (four Mondays in a month) times 9 (nine months working there). Because 4 x 9 is 36 this means Liah has had 36 panic attacks while driving to work.

She then compared what her fears predicted to what actually happened. "I was convinced I was going to be fired. I felt like I was going to pass out, have a "nervous breakdown," or lose control of the car and crash. When I wrote the actual numbers, I realized none of those things has ever happened!" "36 panic attacks. 0 nervous breakdowns. 0 passing out. 0 auto accidents. 0 times I was fired. Wow. 36 to 0. I never looked at it that way. I guess I really do not have to worry about those things."

Create Your Own Fears vs. Facts Table

Use all the approaches explained above. The more facts your Thinking Brain has to work with, the more it can replace fears with facts and untrue or unhelpful thoughts, self-talk, or lessons with statements that are true and helpful.

I encourage you to reread this chapter until you are familiar and comfortable with this skill. Using your Thinking Brain is vital to breaking free of panic.

Using Your Fears vs. Facts

Writing down your fears vs. facts helps you change your thinking. Program this new thinking into your brain by reading—or even better, saying aloud—your fears and the corresponding facts. Read (or say aloud) what you have written in the left column followed by immediately reading or saying what you have written in the right column, going from left to right, one row at a time so you begin to replace fear thoughts with fact-based, helpful thoughts.

Doing this helps build and strengthen new neural pathways in your brain. You are training your brain to switch from panic thinking to logical, fact-

Example: Liah's Fears vs. Facts 1

Fears	Facts	Realistic?
I'll do a bad job at work.	My reviews have all been positive. My boss compliments me all the time. He said, "You did a great job" and "they were glad they hired me."	No
I might get fired.	This is my third job and I've never been fired. This company recruited me out of college because they wanted me to work for them. My work record is good. My boss never said anything about my being close to being fired. I am not on probation and I have not been given any warnings.	No
If I'm not perfect, people won't respect me.	I don't actually know anyone who is "totally perfect." I accept my friends and co-workers despite their imperfections. My friends seem to accept me even when I'm being myself and relaxing. I like people for who they are, not for their grades or the money they make.	No

Example: Liah's Fears vs. Facts 2

Fears	Facts	Realistic?
When I'm having a panic attack, I might lose control.	I have had at least 36 panic attacks and I never lost control. When I panic, I don't pass out, scream or yell. Also, I now know that anxiety doesn't cause anyone to lose control. And, I'm starting to realize that I don't have to ALWAYS be 100% in control of everything. Life does have uncertainties, and I can cope with them.	No
I'll have a nervous breakdown and never recover.	The fact is that anxiety cannot cause me to go crazy, break down, or lose control. After all the panic attacks I have had, if I were going to go crazy or lose control, I would have done it by now.	No
People will be able to tell that I'm having a panic attack. They will see my hands shaking or hear my voice trembling.	Most people cannot tell when others are having a panic attack. Bill said he was having a panic attack in therapy group last week, and nobody in group even knew it! However, even if someone did notice I was anxious, so what? Everybody has anxiety sometimes. My friends and family have been supportive when they know I'm feeling anxious. I will just do my belly breathing and use the skills I've learned.	No

based, coping thinking. You are activating and strengthening your Thinking Brain and preparing it to reassure and override your Reacting Brain.

Read and reread what you have written. Review the facts and the new ways of thinking over and over again. Take your Fears vs. Facts with you. Carry a printout of the table or put it on your smart phone. If you want, take a pack of file cards. Write them a fear on one side and the facts on the other. Do that for each anxiety-triggering statement. Study them like flashcards until you can quickly and convincingly counter each fear with facts.

True Alarm – When the Facts Support Your Fears

Sometimes your fears and the facts agree. When the facts support and confirm your fears, your Reacting Brain is doing its job. It is sending a true alarm. Your Thinking Brain agrees with the Reacting Brain that a real danger exists.

In this case, you have a real-life problem. You need to use helpful thinking and create a plan to prevent or cope with the problem. Here are some examples of true alarms (page 182). Notice that the facts support and agree with the fears.

Responding to a True Alarm

Your Reacting Brain has done its job. Now turn this problem over to your Thinking Brain. Create a realistic coping plan and figure out what to do.

Create a True Alarm Coping Plan

Use Form 11-02: True Alarm Coping Plan (page 184) or make a table with two columns in your computer to make a plan for any of your fears that are realistic.

In the first column, write down those problems that facts say are realistic and likely.

In the second column, fill in what you will do if the feared event happens. Plan how you will avoid, minimize, leave, or cope with this problem. Write down your plan. Then write a back-up plan, a back-up to your back-up, and so on until you have a coping plan for *each likely situation*. Remember you only need a coping plan when the evidence says the feared event is realistic and likely.

Follow Your Coping Plan

Reacting Brain alerted you to a realistic problem. You used your Thinking Brain to get the facts and to create a coping plan. Now follow your plan.

If you are following your plan and you start to worry, reassure your Reacting Brain that you have a plan and are following it. Accept uncertainty as inevitable. Make a note of the worry but postpone worrying about it until your scheduled worry time.

If you are anxious because you are *not following* your plan, start following it, or make a better plan. Your Reacting Brain will keep nagging you until you do. It is doing *its job*. You need to *do yours!*

Example: Fears vs. Facts with True Alarms 1

Fears	Facts	Realistic?
I won't have enough money to pay the bills.	I lost my job 6 months ago. Unemployment runs out this month. I have no income. No one has called me for a job interview. I owe thousands of dollars on my credit cards. My savings and checking accounts are nearly empty. I have a problem. I do not have enough money to pay my bills. I need to do something.	Yes
I'm afraid the tingling in my feet means something is medically wrong with me.	I have had diabetes for years, but never take the medicine the doctor prescribed. When I check my sugar, it is in the 400s or higher. My doctor told me that if I get tingling it could be the sign of a serious problem. I need to take better care of myself.	Yes
I get anxious at night and worry that I am not safe. I have started waking up at night with panic attacks.	My partner hits me, especially when he drinks and he is drinking more and more. Last week, he started punching me when I was asleep and wouldn't stop. I ran out of the house in my nightgown, bleeding. The facts are that he hits me when he drinks, he drinks often, and he hit me when I was asleep. Staying with him is not safe. I need to move out.	Yes

Example: Fears vs. Facts with True Alarms 2

Fears	Facts	Realistic?
I'm afraid of having a heart attack.	I have already had 2 heart attacks. I don't exercise or eat healthy. I have high blood pressure and bad cholesterol and my doctor says I'm going to have another heart attack unless I start taking care of myself. If I don't change, my fear of having another heart attack is very realistic. I need to make changes.	Yes

Example: True Alarm Coping Plan

See page 185 for the coping plans each person developed for the examples of realistic fears on Example: Fears vs. Facts with True Alarms.

False Alarm - When Facts Contradict Your Fears

When the facts contradict your fears, your Reacting Brain is sending a false alarm. You do *not* want to act on your feelings of anxiety or danger. You do *not* want to act on your panic thoughts of fear and danger. You do *not* want to leave or escape, avoid, take unneeded "safety" actions, look out for "danger" that isn't there, or fight the anxiety response because it frightens you. As you learned in Chapter 2 The Anxiety Cycle, these actions only strengthen the anxiety cycle.

You want to *act on the facts*, not your fears. This is the only way to show your Reacting Brain there is no real danger.

Form 11-02: True Alarm Coping Plan

What if …. ? Realistic Likely Problem	Then I will …. Plan to Avoid or Cope with the Problem

Example: True Alarm Coping Plans

What if ....? Realistic Likely Problem	Then I will .... Plan to Avoid or Cope with the Problem
I won't have enough money to pay the bills. The fact is, that I lost my job 6 months ago, and my savings account is nearly empty.	Take a part-time job until I find a full-time job. Go to temp agencies. Go to the Unemployment Office. Apply for food stamps and welfare. Ask relatives for help. Consider filing for bankruptcy.
I'm afraid the tingling in my feet means something is medically wrong. The truth is, that I have diabetes and I'm not taking my medication or watching my diet. My doctor has warned me about this.	Take my medication as prescribed. Call the doctor. Meet with a dietician and diabetes educator. Go to a diabetes class. Make healthy lifestyle changes. Change what I eat. Start exercising.
I'm afraid for my safety at night, and I'm having panic attacks while I sleep. My partner is hitting me, especially at night after drinking and he drinks most nights. He hit me when I was asleep and could have hurt me badly. I need to move out.	Stay with friends or family. Call the local domestic violence shelter and community programs for help getting food, shelter, and a job. Talk with a therapist or healthcare provider who can help. Consider getting a restraining order.
I'm afraid of having a heart attack. I've had 2 heart attacks already, I'm overweight, I don't exercise or eat healthy. My doctor says I'm at high risk for another heart attack unless I take care of my body better.	Take my medication every day. Meet with a nutritionist or dietician. Stop drinking sodas. Eat smaller amounts and healthier foods. Start walking 20-30 minutes after work.

Coping with Uncertainty

After completing your Fears vs. Facts form as described in this chapter, you will usually know whether your Reacting Brain is sending a false alarm or a true alarm as explained above.

However, some situations are not as obviously true or false as those shown above. You may have trouble deciding whether your fears are realistic and likely, or unrealistic and unlikely. For instance, you may worry about your loved ones' safety and have reason to be concerned. Or like Amanda in the story below, you may be facing job uncertainty, financial uncertainty, health issues, or other stresses.

Sometimes, despite getting all the facts, there is uncertainty. Things you fear or worry about may come true or they *may not*. There may be no way to predict with confidence and no way to know for sure. When this is the case, follow these steps:

First, accept that uncertainty is part of life. As you learned in Chapter 9 Reducing External Stress Triggers, accepting reduces the effect of external stress triggers.

Next, think about the fact that absolute certainty in life is impossible. No one ever gets a total guarantee of safety. This has been true for the entire history of the human race. Every person has always lived with this fact. Uncertainty is not the same as danger. It is just the way life is.

Understand that when you are frightened, you want to control or predict what will happen. This is understandable, but not possible. Life is *not* completely predictable; you *cannot* know or control what will happen.

Finally, reflect on the truth that the more you seek or demand certainty, perfection, total control, or absolute guarantees, the more uncertain, anxious, and panicky you will become. On the other hand, the more you accept uncertainty as a natural and inevitable part of life, the less anxious and panicked you will be. This is another paradoxical truth about panic.

For other techniques that can help you with uncertainty, see I am Dealing with Uncertainty in Chapter 14 (page 252).

Story: Amanda

Amanda's boss has said he may have to lay off employees or cut hours if business does not improve. However, he also told Amanda he knew how much her customers liked her and what a great job she was doing. He even confided to her that his mother had raised him on her own, so he appreciated how hard it can be for her as a single parent.

Amanda told us, "I know he likes me. He might fire someone else and hire me for more hours. But what if he has to reduce my hours? Or what if he has to cut everyone's hours? What if he goes out of business? I'm staying awake at night worrying over and over. I'm starting to panic about this."

We agreed that all of those options were possible. Amanda wrote a Fears vs. Facts table and realized she could face a real-life problem so next she wrote a True Alarm Coping Plan. She decided to get more facts ("I'll ask my boss what his plans are and how the business is doing."), to stay in her job but to make back-up plans ("I'll look into job training programs and check the want ads."), and to accept uncertainty ("I like my job right now. Whatever happens in the future, I will deal with it then.").

This Week

Work on evaluating any thoughts that frighten you or act as possible panic triggers. Use facts and logic to decide if these thoughts are realistic, likely, true, and helpful – or not.

Complete your personal Fears vs. Facts table to separate false alarms from true alarms. Then use the table to practice switching from unhelpful fear-based thinking to helpful fact-based thinking.

When facts and logic agree that you face a real problem, create a True Alarm Coping Plan. Then carry out your plan.

When facts and logic cannot resolve your uncertainty about a situation, use the Coping with Uncertainty approach (see page 186).

Notice when you start to act on the *facts* rather than your fear thoughts. Changing your actions is the next step in breaking your anxiety/panic cycle.

Continue to reduce your triggers. Keep filling out your Anxiety and Panic Records. Notice patterns and changes.

Chapter Summary

You have learned how to examine and challenge your fear thoughts by comparing fears with facts. Using this information, you can decide if an alarm is realistic, and make plans or take actions based on the facts. We have also covered ways to deal with situations that are uncertain.

Track your progress using Form 11-99: Completed Chapter 11. Note things you have learned, or been surprised by, in this chapter.

This completes Step 4. Check Form 1-03: Reward Plan (page 16) to see your planned reward for completing this step.

Form 11-99: Completed Chapter 11

Date completed: _____

Lessons learned: _____

_____

Chapter **12:**

Step 5 Learn Anxiety Sensations Are Safe

"Something's turned around for me. My heart starts to pound sometimes, or I'll begin to feel short of breath, and it's sort of uncomfortable, but I'm just not scared of it. I just don't even react to it anymore." — *Amy*

Completing and reviewing your forms and records will help you identify your fears and fight back against them using questions, numbers, facts, and logic. Notice every positive change and sign of progress. You may be starting to view things more realistically. You may be getting better at putting things in perspective and replacing untrue or unhelpful thinking with factual, helpful thinking.

When your Thinking Brain *agrees* with your Reacting Brain that you have a likely real-life problem, you now know how to create a coping plan. And where you face uncertainty, you have better coping tools as well.

What patterns and changes are you noticing in your Anxiety Records and Panic Records? How are you breaking your anxiety cycle?

In this next step, you will use your new skills and knowledge to take control of your life by having your *Thinking Brain* decide what to do when you feel panicky. Having the facts can give you—and your Thinking Brain—the courage to act in ways that break the vicious cycle of anxiety.

A Reacting Brain is good to have, but you don't want a primitive caveman running your life or making major decisions for you, any more than you would let a two-year-old drive your car. *You* should be in the driver's seat of your life.

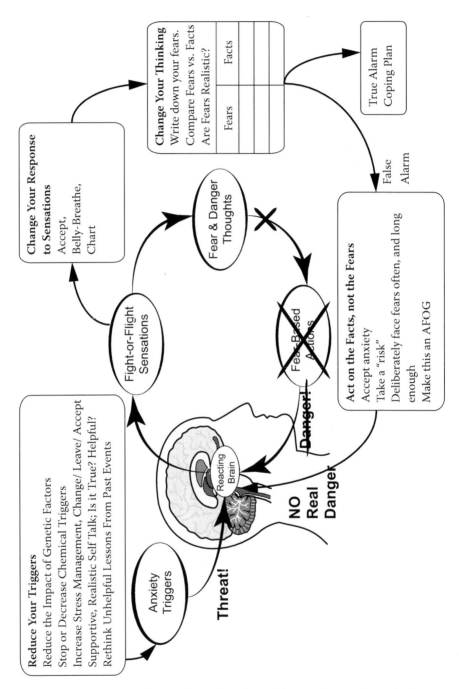

Figure 12-01: Learning Anxiety Sensations Are Safe

Figure 12-02: Don't let your Reacting Brain take over

Act on Facts, Not Fears

Facts and logic will convince your rational, logical, verbal Thinking Brain that you are safe and can cope. They will *not* convince your Reacting Brain. Your primitive caveman brain needs to be *shown*.

Your Reacting Brain *learns from experience* more than from words. So, once it has mistakenly decided that a situation, activity, or sensation is dangerous to you, the ONLY way it can learn that that situation, activity, or sensation is *not* dangerous is by confronting it and seeing for itself that the danger it fears does not exist.

This process of correcting the Reacting Brain's mistaken fears faces two obstacles:

- First, your caveman brain is designed to remember *danger*, not safety, so it may take *several* experiences of confronting the (nonexistent) danger to prove to the Reacting Brain that you are safe.

- Second, because its job is to protect you, it will be very, very, very reluctant to take the "risk" of confronting "danger".

At this point your Thinking Brain takes over and plays an important role. Together you and your Thinking Brain must override the Reacting Brain's instinctive response.

Your Thinking Brain is like the rational, loving but firm, adult parent while your Reacting Brain is more like an overtired, irrational, screaming toddler. You need to ally with your Thinking Brain because, really, which part of your brain knows best?

Facts and logic help your Thinking Brain decide when the Reacting Brain is sending a false alarm. They also give your Thinking Brain the *courage it needs* to drag your Reacting Brain—kicking and screaming—into situations the Reacting Brain thinks are dangerous—and force it to *stay* in these situations long enough for your caveman brain to calm down, pay attention, and realize there is no danger.

This is the final, most powerful step in breaking the anxiety cycle. Here are guidelines to follow:

- Act on the *facts*, not your fears.

- *Deliberately* face your fears.

- Face fears *often* enough and *long* enough for your Reacting Brain to learn that what it thought was dangerous is not.

- Take what your Reacting Brain thinks is a "*risk*."

- *Accept* anxiety. It means your Reacting Brain is paying attention and can learn something!

When your fears tell you one thing, and the facts tell you something different, use the facts to give your Thinking Brain the courage to override your Reacting Brain. <u>Act on the facts, despite your fear thoughts.</u>

Deliberately Face Your Fears

If you *only face* a feared situation, activity, or sensation when you cannot avoid it, your Reacting Brain will think, "Whew. You made it through that time, but don't press your luck!" It knows you were afraid and did not face the situation, activity, or sensation out of choice. The Reacting Brain concludes that the situation, activity, or sensation is a threat and becomes *more likely* to trigger the fight-or-flight response the next time the situation appears.

This explains why you may have faced a fear, or experienced past panic attacks, but are still afraid of them. You did what I call "white-knuckling it through." You faced it because you had to and focused on enduring or surviving. You may have also been fighting the panic response or taking fear-based actions. You probably got away from the situation as quickly as you could with a shudder of relief. Obviously, this *is not* the most effective way to convince your Reacting Brain that these situations are safe.

You want to face your fears by choice. <u>Choose your actions based on facts, despite fear.</u>

Facing Fears Long Enough and Often

When you do deliberately face fears, it is most helpful to stay long enough and to face them often enough for the Reacting Brain to truly learn "There is no real danger." Deliberately facing a fear *long enough* means giving your caveman brain time to calm down, look around, and see that you—and the situation—are safe.

Deliberately facing a fear *often enough* means giving your caveman brain repeated opportunities to learn and remember that you and the situation are safe. Since this part of your brain is designed to learn danger—not safety—learning takes repeated experiences.

The take home message is: *deliberately face your fears long enough and often enough for the Reacting Brain to calm down, or even get bored.* This helps you learn new lessons and create new nerve pathways in the brain that can override the old, mistaken lessons.

The Fastest Way to Overcome Fear

Research suggests that the fastest way to get over a fear is to confront the fear for **one to three hours at a time, several times a week**.

This may be the best, fastest, and most powerful way to break the panic cycle. This is like jumping into the deep end of the pool. You get it over with fast.

Facing fears long and often gives your brain and body lots of time to calm down, realize you are safe, and even get bored. Boredom has benefits; it is hard to feel terrified when you're bored!

The Second Fastest Way to Overcome Fear

If you are not able to practice for one to three hours several times a week, the next best plan is to schedule shorter practice sessions every week. Decide in advance how long you will face your fear.

This is like easing into the shallow end of the pool and waiting for your body to adjust to the temperature before going into deeper water. This method takes longer, but it does work, and some people prefer it. Ideally, stay in the situation until your fear goes down so your Reacting Brain has time to learn that you are safe.

A Third Way to Overcome Fear

Grab every chance you get to face your fears for as long as you can. Take every opportunity that becomes available. Try to create ways to face your fears as you go about your week.

If you tried this approach of waiting for spontaneous chances to face fears and/or you tried the second fastest approach (scheduling short practice sessions) and you are still afraid, bite the bullet and arrange several 1-3-hour practice sessions each week.

It usually takes *much less time than you expect* to overcome fears once you begin actively facing them using the knowledge and tools you have learned. Keep rereading this book and using your Fears vs. Facts to strengthen your Thinking Brain.

Take "Risks"

Keep in mind what you have learned about your Reacting Brain. It can believe things are more dangerous than they are. It can be well-intentioned, but misinformed. Listening to it can be like following directions given by someone who is looking at the wrong map.

History provides a wonderful example of how we can believe things are dangerous when they aren't. Centuries ago, when most of the world's oceans were unexplored, people thought the far-off seas were dangerous places where dragons lived. Ancient maps carried the warning, "Here be dragons!" Only after courageous sailors sailed into those "dangerous, dragon-filled waters" did they learn that the map was wrong. No dragons! No danger!

Your Reacting Brain acts based on what it believes. Its "map" may show "dragons and dangers" where none exist. You need to update its map and the only way to do that is to *show* it. Drag your caveman brain into the "dangerous waters" and show it: "Look! No dragons! No danger!"

Accept Anxiety

When you act on the facts and face your fears, your Reacting Brain will not be happy at first! It will send its usual false alarm and trigger full or partial panic. In this situation, feeling panicky or anxious is good. It is a sign that you are doing the right thing.

Anxiety means your Reacting Brain is paying attention and thinks you are doing something dangerous. You are giving your Reacting Brain a chance to learn that you are *not* in danger and that it does *not* need to "protect" you.

Each time the Reacting Brain's old programming is activated ("This is dangerous"), you have a chance to override it and update your bodyguard brain's "map" ("Oh, this is *not* as dangerous as I thought.").

If you feel anxious or panicky as you face your fears, keep going. You are doing the right thing. Good work. Go for it!

Liah told us, "I just say 'Bring it on!' And the anxiety quickly starts to go away."

AFOG: Another F____ Opportunity for Growth!

If you are like most of my clients, you will find the concept of AFOG to be really important and helpful. It gives you a new way of looking at life's challenges, including unneeded panic.

AFOG (pronounced A-fog) is short for **A**nother "**F**_____" **O**pportunity for **G**rowth. I translate the F in that phrase as 'Fabulous' or 'Fantastic'. In real life, many clients translate it using another "F***" word! Translate the "F" in AFOG any way you like.

Each episode of anxiety or panic is a golden opportunity to practice new skills, to give your Reacting Brain new experiences, and to override old lessons and replace them with new ones. Each episode of panic or anxiety is an AFOG.

Because your Reacting Brain learns from experience, not words, you have to *show* it that you are safe and no danger threatens. To convince it to stop protecting you, it has to see that you can repeatedly face the "danger" without being harmed.

Experience is **the only way** it learns "*There is <u>NO</u> REAL DANGER.*"

Since its job is to learn danger, not safety, you have to show it repeatedly. You are overriding old learning. You are creating new connections within your brain.

Your first step was putting your fears into words and getting the facts. When the facts say that panic thoughts are untrue and/or unhelpful and that the Reacting Brain is sending a false alarm, you need to *act on the facts*.

If your actions contradict your words, your Reacting Brain believes *what you do*, not what you say. So, you cannot avoid, leave, stay hypervigilant (on the lookout for danger), take safety actions, or take fear-based actions. If you *say* you are safe, but *act* like you are not, your bodyguard will believe your actions, not your words.

This is why your Thinking Brain must consider your fears and worries thoroughly and logically. It needs to know that although panic can be uncomfortable and unwanted, it is *not* dangerous, there is *no* serious danger, and the panic response just *misfired* because of one or more triggers.

To recap: information gives your Thinking Brain the courage to override your Reacting Brain—to drag it kicking and screaming into facing things it thinks are dangerous—and make it stay there and pay attention long enough to calm down and learn that there is no danger.

Learning Anxiety Sensations Are Safe

In this step, you teach your Reacting Brain that anxiety or panic sensations are harmless. Since your Reacting Brain only learns from repeated experience, you will teach it by doing physical exercises that create bodily sensations similar to those that occur when you panic.

Figure 12-03: Help your Reacting Brain learn safety

"Wait, what?!," I hear you say. "Why do I want to do that?!?"

You want to do this because creating the physical sensations of panic, watching them subside, and repeating the process over and over, makes these feelings familiar and no longer threatening. Panic will never feel nice, but it no longer has to scare you.

Why This Is Worth Doing – It Works!

"I kept doing the exercises and they got easier." – Jessie

"It was scary at first but then I realized that nothing bad happened. Feelings that used to scare me don't anymore." – Kat

It is hard to be scared by a physical sensation after you have deliberately created it–time and again–over and over–until you are bored by it. You will practice these exercises until the panic symptoms they create become boringly familiar.

These physical exercises can *really work*; even if you are nervous about doing them at first. It may take a little time and practice, but the results are worth it. I promise.

I have done all these exercises alongside hundreds of clients over many years. I know from personal experience, from my clients, and from the published research, that these exercises can make an important difference. They really help.

Physical Exercises: First Practice

Start by doing *each* exercise *only <u>one</u> time*. This is how you identify which exercises will be most helpful for retraining your Reacting Brain.

You can do this first practice on your own, or you may want to have someone practice with you, such as a friend or a therapist who is helping you get over panic. It is reassuring to have company and the other person can help by keeping track of time. If no one is available to time you, use a kitchen timer or a timer app on your phone (part of the clock app on iPhone).

If you worry that any of these exercises are not medically safe for you, check with your primary healthcare provider before doing the exercise. Describe the exercise to your healthcare professional and get their medical okay.

Preparing for Physical Exercises First Practice

You will need:

- A drinking straw for the Straw Breathing exercise.
- A chair that spins or enough space to stand and spin for the Spinning exercise.
- A mirror for the Staring in Mirror exercise.

If you are using paper forms you will need:

- The Form 12-01: Physical Exercises First Practice form (page 200)
- A pen or pencil.
- Watch, clock, kitchen timer, or a timer app on a phone or tablet.

Physical Exercises First Practice Instructions

If you are using the paper version of Form 12-01: Physical Exercises First Practice you can ignore the first column ("Subsequent Practice") for now; you will fill it in later.

Do *each* of the first seven exercises *only one time*. The last two exercises are optional, and you can do them if you would like.

Read all the information about each exercise *before* doing it, including any warnings. Then follow the instructions and do the exercise one time.

Immediately after each exercise:

* Rate the *highest level of anxiety* you felt during or after the exercise on a scale of 0-10. Record your rating in the column for Anxiety.

* Rate *how similar* the physical sensations are to body sensations you experience when you are anxious or panicky using the same 0-10 scale. Note this in the Similar to Panic column.

* Write a word or two in the Sensations column summarizing the physical sensations you experienced during this exercise.

Form 12-01: Physical Exercises First Practice

```
0-----1------2------3------4------5------6------7------8------9-------10
```
| None | Mild | Medium | Strong | Worst |

Subs Practice	Physical Exercise	Anxiety 0-10	Similar to Panic 0-10	Sensa-tions
	Running in Place			
	Spinning			
	Balloon Breathing			
	Straw Breathing			
	Staring at Wall			
	Staring in Mirror			
	Head Lift			
	Muscle Tensing			
	Tight Throat (optional)			
	Hot, Sweating, Flushing (optional)			

Running in Place

Warning

Do not do this exercise if it causes pain or if a healthcare provider or a physical therapist has told you not to run.

Instructions

Run in place as fast as you can for one minute. *If you are unable to run,* replace this with any activity that raises your heart rate, such as marching in place and lifting your legs up high, or sitting on a chair and moving your arms and legs rapidly.

Pay attention to your body. Notice the sensations in your body.

Sensations

The purpose is to create sensations of a fast pounding heart, palpitations, sweating, and feeling short of breath.

Rating

Under Anxiety, record the number that reflects the highest level of anxiety you felt *during* the exercise or *just after stopping*. Use the 0-10 scale. How much did these feelings scare you? Some people feel most anxious just after stopping this exercise.

If the sensations did not scare you, but you think they *would* scare you if they came as part of a panic attack, use *that* number as your rating.

Under Similar to Panic, use the 0-10 scale to record how similar these physical feelings are to those you get when you panic.

Under Sensations, briefly write the physical sensations you felt during or after this exercise. Did you feel short of breath? Did your heart race? Record the major bodily sensations created by this exercise, even if they are different from the ones listed.

Spinning

If you get dizzy when you are anxious, this exercise may be particularly helpful for you.

Warning

If your stomach gets upset on winding roads or amusement park rides or if this exercise makes you queasy, turn more slowly and/or for a shorter time.

If you have Meniere's disease, other inner ear problems, or any illness that affects your balance, check with your healthcare provider before doing this exercise.

Instructions

Stand and turn. Another option is to sit in a chair that can turn in a circle. You will spin around for one minute, completing _one turn every three seconds_.

First, set the pace by taking three seconds to make one complete turn. Time the three seconds using a clock or by counting "one thousand one, one thousand two, one thousand three." As you can see, this is a moderate pace. You are not trying to imitate a tornado!

Spin at that pace for one minute.

Pay attention to your body. Notice the sensations in your body as you spin and after you stop turning.

Sensations

The purpose is to create sensations of dizziness, visual changes, and sometimes brief, mild, temporary queasiness.

Rating

Under Anxiety, use the 0-10 scale to record the highest level of anxiety you felt doing this exercise or just after stopping. How much did these feelings scare you?

If the sensations did not scare you, but you think they _would_ scare you if they came as part of a panic attack, use _that_ number as your rating.

Under Similar to Panic, use the 0-10 scale to record how similar these physical feelings are to those you get when you panic.

Under Sensations, record the physical changes or body sensations you noticed.

Balloon Breathing

Warning

If you have asthma, lung disease, breathing difficulties, heart disease, seizures, or epilepsy, check with your healthcare provider before doing this exercise.

Instructions

Sit down and breathe for one minute as if you were blowing up a balloon. Take a deep belly breath. Blow out slowly and steadily. Put your fist or your fingers to your mouth as if you were actually holding a balloon.

Steady, sustained, deep breaths are usually enough to cause the sensations you want. You do not have to create gale-force winds. You are not trying to blow the house down!

If you have no sensations after 30 seconds, blow out faster or with more force until you create sensations.

Pay close attention to your body. Notice the sensations in your body.

Sensations

The purpose of this exercise is to create feelings of tingling, cold or hot, shortness of breath, dry throat, unreality, and/or dizziness. Sometimes headache or other feelings may occur.

Rating

Under Anxiety, record the highest level of anxiety (0-10) you felt doing this exercise or just after stopping. How much did these feelings scare you?

If the sensations did not scare you, but you think they *would* scare you if they came as part of a panic attack, use *that* number as your rating.

Under Similar to Panic, record how similar (0-10) these physical feelings are to those you get when you panic.

Under Sensations, write the physical changes or body sensations you noticed.

Straw Breathing

Instructions

Pinch your nose closed and breathe through a drinking straw for one minute.

If this creates no sensations after 20 seconds, bite down a little on the straw to make the opening smaller.

If you feel you must stop before the minute is up, try to continue for just five seconds beyond the time when you first want to stop. Record how many seconds you did the straw breathing.

Pay attention to what happens in your body. Notice the sensations in your body.

Sensations

The purpose is to create feelings of shortness of breath, suffocating, or not getting enough air.

Rating

Under Anxiety, record the highest level of anxiety (0-10) you felt doing this exercise or just after stopping. How much did these feelings scare you?

If the sensations did not scare you, but you think they *would* scare you if they came as part of a panic attack, use *that* number as your rating.

Under Similar to Panic, record how similar (0-10) these physical feelings are to those you get when you panic.

Under Sensations, write the physical changes or body sensations you noticed.

If you stopped before the full minute was up, record the number of seconds you breathed through the straw. When you practice this exercise, start out practicing for just that length of time until it no longer frightens you. Gradually extend your straw breathing time until you can do it for one minute without fear.

Staring at Wall

Instructions

Set a timer for this exercise so you won't be distracted by looking at the clock.

Pick a spot on the wall and stare at it for two minutes. Focus on the spot and notice any visual changes. Blinking is OK.

Sensations

The purpose is to create visual changes and a sense of unreality, as if you are not quite there, or as if things outside are not quite real.

Staring fixedly at one place is particularly good for creating blurriness, visual spots, moving in and out of focus, and other visual changes.

Rating

Under Anxiety, record the highest level of anxiety (0-10) you felt doing this exercise or just after stopping. How much did these feelings scare you?

If the sensations did not scare you, but you think they *would* scare you if they came as part of a panic attack, use *that* number as your rating.

Under Similar to Panic, record how similar (0-10) these physical feelings are to those you get when you panic.

Under Sensations, write the body sensations you noticed.

Staring in a Mirror

Instructions

Set a timer for this exercise so you won't be distracted by looking at the clock.

Stare at yourself in a mirror for two minutes. Notice any changes in your vision. Pay attention to any other sensations.

Sensations

Staring into a mirror helps create a sense of unreality and being out of your body or disconnected from your body. This can be good for fears of "going crazy."

Rating

Under Anxiety, record the highest level of anxiety (0-10) you felt doing this exercise or just after stopping. How much did these feelings scare you?

If the sensations did not scare you, but you think they *would* scare you if they came as part of a panic attack, use *that* number as your rating.

Under Similar to Panic, record how similar (0-10) these physical feelings are to those you get when you panic.

Under Sensations, write the body sensations you noticed.

Head Lift

Warning

If you have neck or back problems, do not cause yourself pain or injury. If you have very low blood pressure or get lightheaded when you stand up quickly (postural hypotension), you may want to raise your head a little less quickly.

Instructions

Sit down and spread your legs apart so you can put your head between your knees. Put your head as far down as you can, hold that position for 30 seconds, then sit up quickly. Pay close attention to your body and notice all the sensations during this exercise and after you stop.

Sensations

The purpose is to create sensations of heaviness in the head and feeling the blood pounding in the head while your head is down. After sitting up, the purpose is to create sensations of lightheadedness, dizziness, or a feeling of blood rushing away from your head.

Rating

Under Anxiety, record the highest level of anxiety (0-10) you felt doing this exercise or just after stopping. How much did these feelings scare you?

If the sensations did not scare you, but you think they *would* scare you if they came as part of a panic attack, use *that* number as your rating.

Under Similar to Panic, record how similar (0-10) these physical feelings are to those you get when you panic.

Under Sensations, write the body sensations you noticed.

Muscle Tensing

Warning

Do not cause yourself pain.

If you wear contact lenses, do not squeeze your eyes. If you have long fingernails, do not dig your nails into your hand. If tensing causes pain in certain joints or muscles, only tense the other muscles.

Instructions

Tense every part of your body for one minute.

Here are three ways to do this exercise. Pick any one:

1. Sit in a chair. Hold your arms and legs out and tense all your muscles from your toes to your face for one minute.

2. In a sturdy chair with armrests, put your heels on the floor and lift yourself off the chair by pushing down with your hands on the armrests. Hold this position tensing all your muscles for one minute.

3. Hold a push-up, or a plank position, with your feet on the floor and your weight on your arms, tensing all your muscles for one minute.

Pay attention to your body. Notice the sensations in your body.

Sensations

The purpose is to create sensations of muscle tension, shakiness, trembling, or a feeling of weakness.

Rating

Under Anxiety, record the highest level of anxiety (0-10) you felt doing this exercise or just after stopping. How much did these feelings scare you?

If the sensations did not scare you, but you think they *would* scare you if they came as part of a panic attack, use *that* number as your rating.

Under Similar to Panic, record how similar (0-10) these physical feelings are to those you get when you panic.

Under Sensations, write the body sensations you noticed.

Tight Throat (Optional)

If your throat gets tight, or you have feelings of choking or a lump your throat when you get anxious, practice this exercise.

Instructions

Here are two ways to do this exercise:

1. Swallow 5 times as fast as possible. Swallow as hard and fast as you can. Force yourself to keep swallowing without a break. Start swallowing now: Swallow 1 - Swallow 2 - Swallow 3 - Swallow 4 - Swallow 5

2. Pull your collar around your throat or push gently against the lower part of your throat with your fingers, for one minute.

Notice the sensations in your throat. Pay attention to your body.

Sensations

The purpose is to create sensations of feeling unable to swallow, throat tightness, throat closing, lump in the throat, or muscle tension in the throat.

Rating

Under Anxiety, record the highest level of anxiety (0-10) you felt doing this exercise or just after stopping. How much did these feelings scare you?

If the sensations did not scare you, but you think they *would* scare you if they came as part of a panic attack, use *that* number as your rating.

Under Similar to Panic, record how similar (0-10) these physical feelings are to those you get when you panic.

Under Sensations, write the body sensations you noticed.

Hot, Sweating, Flushing (Optional)

If you get hot, sweaty, or flushed when you feel anxious, practice one or more of these exercises.

Instructions

There are several ways to practice. Find the one most appropriate for you.

1. Wearing warm clothes, a heavy sweater and your warmest coat, sit in the sun, by a heater, or in the car with the heater on for about five minutes. **Warning: Do <u>not</u> run the car engine in a garage or other enclosed space!** Doing this can fill the area with carbon monoxide and kill you.

2. Sit in the bathroom in warm clothes and run the shower with the hottest water for about five minutes. Breathe in the steam.

3. Go to a gym or spa and use the steam room or sauna for about five minutes. Follow the safety instructions when using a steam room or sauna.

Pay attention to your body. Notice the sensations in your body.

Sensations

The purpose is to create sensations of being overheated, sweaty, flushed, or unable to breathe.

Rating

Under Anxiety, record the highest level of anxiety you felt doing this exercise or just after stopping. How much did these feelings scare you?

If the sensations did not scare you, but you think they *would* scare you if they came as part of a panic attack, use *that* number as your rating.

Under Similar to Panic, record how similar (0-10) these physical feelings are to those you get when you panic.

Under Sensations, write the body sensations you noticed.

Story: Raj

Raj found that these exercises triggered different reactions, as do many people. Some exercises (like Spinning) created a lot of anxiety, while others (like Staring) created very little anxiety. Some of the sensations created by the exercises were very similar to his spontaneous panic sensations (nausea from Spinning); others were only slightly similar to his naturally occurring anxiety sensations (shakiness from Muscle Tensing).

Example: Raj's Physical Exercises First Practice

```
0-----1------2------3------4------5------6------7------8------9-------10
None        Mild         Medium        Strong        Worst
```

Subs Practice	Physical Exercise	Anxiety 0-10	Similar to Panic 0-10	Sensa-tions
	Running in Place	7	8	*Heart racing, sweating*
	Spinning	8	9	*Dizzy, a little queasy, unreality*
	Balloon Breathing	4	5	*Tingling, dry throat*
	Straw Breathing	3	3	*short of air, suffocating*
	Staring at Wall	0	0	*Boredom*
	Staring in Mirror	0	0	*slightly unreal*
	Head Lift	5	5	*slightly nauseous*
	Muscle Tensing	2	2	*shaky, trembling*
	Tight Throat (optional)	7	7	*Choking, like going to gag*
	Hot, Sweating, Flushing (optional)	5	6	*sweating, short of breath*

Story: Carlos

Like many people, Carlos was anxious about doing these exercises the first time. He had done a lot of work up to this point to challenge his panic thoughts, but his Reacting Brain was still convinced that his physical sensations could lead to a heart attack. Carlos gathered his courage and did the exercises with his wife's help. She did them with him.

What if ALL the exercises scare me?

Not to worry. That means this part of the program will be extremely helpful for you. It proves that you are on the right track.

Tackle them one at a time. Each one will be an AFOG: Another F<u>**!?!</u> (Fabulous?) Opportunity for Growth. Each bit of progress will create ever-widening ripples of positive change, confidence, and freedom.

What if NONE of the exercises scare me?

There are two common reasons why none of the exercises scare you.

One possible explanation is that you are completely over your fear of panic and anxiety. If anxiety or panic sensations truly *no longer* frighten you, if you *no longer* have panic thoughts, and if you are *not* taking any fear-based actions, you may have broken your anxiety cycle already. Reduce your triggers to a minimum. Enjoy your success. Congratulations!

The other possible explanation is that you accidentally did something that interfered with the purpose and effectiveness of the exercises. Here are four likely possibilities and suggestions for each. Did you:

1. **Distract yourself or avoid paying attention to sensations?**
   Repeat the exercises. Stay focused on the physical sensations in your body during and immediately after each exercise. Do not distract.

2. **Take anti-anxiety medicine?**
   Anti-anxiety medication can interfere in three ways. First, the medicine may prevent the sensations from being created. Obviously, your brain cannot learn that sensations are harmless if you do not feel the sensations. Second, many anti-anxiety medicines can interfere with learning. Third, taking a pill before the exercise to prevent panic is

Example: Carlos' Physical Exercises First Practice

```
0-----1------2------3------4------5------6------7------8------9-------10
None        Mild          Medium        Strong         Worst
```

Subs Practice	Physical Exercise	Anxiety 0-10	Similar to Panic 0-10	Sensa-tions
	Running in Place	9	9	*Heart pounding, sweating, hot flash*
	Spinning	3	4	*slightly dizzy*
	Balloon Breathing	6	7	*Dizzy, tingling, unreal*
	Straw Breathing	4	2	*short of breath*
	Staring at Wall	1	2	*Visual changes/ blurriness*
	Staring in Mirror	0	0	*Nothing*
	Head Lift	6	8	*Blood pounding in head*
	Muscle Tensing	5	5	*Trembling, weak feeling*
	Tight Throat (optional)	7	8	*Choking, lump in throat*
	Hot, Sweating, Flushing (optional)	9	9	*sweating, hot flash*

a safety action. You know that safety actions tend to strengthen the anxiety cycle, making you more likely to continue to experience and fear panic.

Repeat the exercises without taking the medicine beforehand.

If you take anti-anxiety medicine on a daily basis, try to do the exercises just before your next scheduled dose. Check with your healthcare provider if you have any questions. Do not make any changes in taking your prescribed medication without checking with your healthcare provider first.

3. **Tell yourself you were safe for some reason?**
   Did you think something like, "It is safe to do these exercises because someone is with me," or "I will be OK because I am near a hospital," or "The sensations are safe because I am bringing them on deliberately, but they are dangerous when they happen out of the blue," or similar thoughts?

   Repeat the exercises without thinking these thoughts. Focus on the feelings in your body. Think about your fears while doing the exercises. Change where you do the exercises.

   Another option is to rate your fear based on how anxious the sensations would make you if you were not in a "safe setting" or if they came on spontaneously as part of a panic attack.

4. **Feel no bodily sensations from some exercises?**
   Repeat those exercises more strongly or for a longer time. The purpose is to create physical sensations in your body.

What if these sensations are not like your panic feelings?

If your anxiety sensations frighten you but none of the exercises created similar sensations, you may need some different exercises. One option is to think about which sensations feel dangerous to you and then find ways to create similar bodily sensations.

Another option is to skip ahead and begin real life practice, see Chapter 13: Learn Activities Are Safe.

Planning Subsequent Practice

Good news! In terms of your physical exercises, the worst is over after the First Practice. For Subsequent Practice, you only need to practice *one exercise* at a time <u>and</u> it will be the exercise with your *lowest anxiety rating*—the exercise that scared you *the least*.

You will practice just this one exercise until it no longer scares you. After that, you will practice the exercise with the *next lowest anxiety rating*. You will practice just *that* one exercise until it no longer scares you, and so on.

Plus, you may not need to practice all the exercises. Only the exercises that created sensations similar to panic are used in your Subsequent Practice Plan.

Create Your Subsequent Practice Plan

If you completed the paper version of Form 12-01: Physical Exercises First Practice earlier, you will now reuse this form to create your Subsequent Practice Plan. This is where you fill in the first column on the left ("Subsequent Practice") following the instructions below.

Follow these steps:

- Put an X in the Subsequent Practice column for any exercise(s) that did *not* make you anxious <u>and</u> did *not* create sensations similar to panic. You do not need to practice these, so they don't get a number.

- Find the exercise with the <u>lowest</u> anxiety rating. Put a 1 in the Subsequent Practice column.

- Put a 2 in the Subsequent Practice column for the exercise with the *next* lowest anxiety rating.

- Continue this process until all exercises that created panic-like sensations have a number in the Subsequent Practice column.

- *If two or more exercises have the <u>same</u> anxiety rating*, decide which exercise would scare you *less* to practice and give that exercise the next number. The other exercise(s) would get the next number(s) in order.

Your list of exercises for subsequent practice may be as short as one exercise or as long as ten exercises. *Only* those exercises that caused anxiety *and* created sensations similar to your anxiety or panic sensations get numbers under Subsequent Practice and become part of your subsequent practice plan.

For example, if you tried both Staring exercises <u>and</u> the two optional exercises (Tight Throat and Hot, Sweating, Flushing), making a total of ten exercises, <u>and</u> *all* exercises created sensations similar to panic <u>and</u> *all* of them created anxiety, you will have ten exercises to practice and the Subsequent Practice column will have numbers from 1 to 10.

If only *five* exercises created sensations similar to panic <u>and</u> created anxiety, you will have five exercises to practice. These five physical exercises will be numbered 1 to 5 under Subsequent Practice. The other exercises will have an X.

Story: Raj

Here is Raj's Physical Exercises First Practice form after he filled in the Subsequent Practice column. Use this example to check that you understand how to fill out this form.

Raj had two sets of exercises that triggered the *same* level of anxiety: Hot, Sweating, Flushing and Head Lift both created a level 5 anxiety; Running in Place and Tight Throat both created a level 7 anxiety. He decided he would rather practice Head Lift before going on to practice Hot, Sweating, Flushing so he gave Head Lift a Subsequent Practice number of 4 and Hot, Sweating, Flushing a Subsequent Practice number of 5. Since he preferred to practice Tight Throat before practicing Running in Place, Tight Throat was given number 6 in the Subsequent Practice form and Running in Place became number 7.

Story: Carlos

Carlos' Physical Exercises First Practice form after he filled in the Subsequent Practice column is on page 219.

Subsequent Practice

Practice is an incredibly important and powerful learning experience. The more often you create these sensations and become familiar with them, the more opportunities your caveman Reacting Brain has to learn that these sensations are safe. Do each exercise until it bores you!

Example: Raj's Physical Exercises First Practice

0-----1------2------3------4------5------6------7------8------9-------10
None   Mild   Medium   Strong   Worst

Subs Practice	Physical Exercise	Anxiety 0-10	Similar to Panic 0-10	Sensa- tions
7	Running in Place	7	8	Heart racing, sweating
8	Spinning	8	9	Dizzy, a little queasy, unreality
3	Balloon Breathing	4	5	Tingling, dry throat
2	Straw Breathing	3	3	Short of air, suffocating
X	Staring at Wall	0	0	Boredom
X	Staring in Mirror	0	0	slightly unreal
4	Head Lift	5	5	slightly nauseous
1	Muscle Tensing	2	2	shaky, trembling
6	Tight Throat (optional)	7	7	Choking, like going to gag
5	Hot, Sweating, Flushing (optional)	5	6	sweating, short of breath

Anxiety often drops *much more quickly* than you expect. Hundreds of people have done these exercises safely and successfully. This is your path to freedom from panic.

Practice starts with the lowest anxiety exercise and progresses gradually as you master each exercise and become familiar with the sensations.

Start with your first exercise:

• If you are using paper forms, look at your Form 12-01: Physical Exercises First Practice form and find number "1" in the Subsequent Practice column. This is your first exercise to practice.

During your subsequent practice time, you will repeat just that *first, lowest-anxiety* exercise five times, pausing between repetitions to let any sensations subside. The goal is to have one practice session a day during which you repeat *one* exercise up to five times until your anxiety rating drops down to a 0 or 1.

After the sensations created by *that first* exercise no longer scare you, you can move on to the *next* exercise on your list and begin to practice that exercise during subsequent practice. Follow the same rules.

If you have practiced one exercise five times and your anxiety rating is still 2 or higher, you are done for the day. Pat yourself on the back and go do something nice for yourself. The next day, start with the *same* exercise and repeat it until your anxiety rating is 0 or 1—or until you have practiced it five times.

Repeat this process until your anxiety rating for that exercise is 0 or 1. Then move to the exercise with the next higher number under Subsequent Practice on your Physical Exercises First Practice form. Practice *that* exercise following the same rules: repeat five times per day or until your anxiety rating is 0 or 1.

Work your way through the exercises *one by one, from least scary to most scary,* one exercise at a time. Do *not* progress to a more challenging exercise until the *current* exercise no longer scares you.

Example: Carlos' Physical Exercises First Practice

0-----1------2------3------4------5------6------7------8------9-------10
None   Mild   Medium   Strong   Worst

Subs Practice	Physical Exercise	Anxiety 0-10	Similar to Panic 0-10	Sensa-tions
9	Running in Place	9	9	Heart pounding, sweating, hot flash
2	Spinning	3	4	slightly dizzy
5	Balloon Breathing	6	7	Dizzy, tingling, unreal
3	Straw Breathing	4	2	short of breath
1	Staring at Wall	1	2	Visual changes/blurriness
X	Staring in Mirror	0	0	Nothing
6	Head Lift	6	8	Blood pounding in head
4	Muscle Tensing	5	5	Trembling, weak feeling
7	Tight Throat (optional)	7	8	Choking, lump in throat
8	Hot, Sweating, Flushing (optional)	9	9	Sweating, hot flash

Using the Physical Exercise Subsequent Practice Form

If you are using paper forms, follow these instructions.

Use Form 12-02: Physical Exercise Subsequent Practice to track your practices and to see your progress:

- Write today's date in the Date column.

- Write the name of the exercise you will practice in the Physical Exercise column.

- Write "1" in the Practice column, because this is your first practice of the day.

- Do the exercise one time and record your maximum anxiety during or shortly after the exercise using the 0-10 scale in the Anxiety column.

- Notice any fear thoughts. Remind yourself of the facts. Calm your body using low and slow belly breathing (see page 147).

- After the sensations subside, do your second practice. Write "2" under Practice and repeat the exercise. Rate your Anxiety after doing the exercise this time. Challenge any fearful thoughts and calm your body.

- Repeat this process for your third, fourth, and fifth practice for that day's subsequent practice session.

- Practice just *one* exercise until either your anxiety rating drops to 0 or 1, *or* you have practiced it five times that day.

- If your anxiety drops to 0 or 1 after fewer than five practices, you may move ahead and start practicing the next exercise on your list.

Story: Raj

Raj's Physical Exercise Subsequent Practice forms are on page 224. He charted 5 days of subsequent practice sessions (from August 11 – August 15). He was delighted to see his anxiety ratings drop within days.

Form 12-2: Physical Exercise Subsequent Practice

0-----1------2------3------4------5------6------7------8------9-------10
None   Mild   Medium   Strong   Worst

Date	Physical Exercise	Practice 0-5	Anxiety 0-10	What are you learning

Story: Carlos

Carlos' Physical Exercise Subsequent Practice forms are on page 226. He started with "Staring at Wall" because that was his least feared activity. He was quickly able to move on to "Spinning" because his anxiety level dropped to 0 after just 3 practices. He worked his way through his list of exercises, practicing each one until his anxiety score was 0 or 1. Carlos was impressed that his anxiety level went down much more quickly than he had expected.

Story: Liah

Liah was very anxious when I explained this part of the treatment to her. "Why would I want to *make* myself panic?" she asked. She reviewed the facts about panic symptoms (that they are uncomfortable but not dangerous) and worked up the courage to try. She felt a tremendous sense of accomplishment after completing the Physical Exercises First Practice form. "I did it!" she exclaimed with pride.

After that first experience, Liah was dedicated to doing subsequent practice. The Physical Exercises Subsequent Practice form showed her that her anxiety ratings went down with each practice. The progress motivated her to continue facing her fears. After a short time, Liah was no longer scared by her physical symptoms. She knew they were not going to harm her and that she had the ability to cope with them. Liah is happy to report that she no longer wakes up in the night with panic attacks, and her drive to work on Monday mornings is panic-free.

This Week

Devote a week or more to subsequent practice, depending on your needs. This is one of the best ways to teach your caveman Reacting Brain that the physical sensations of panic and anxiety are not dangerous and to overcome your fear of them.

Keep updating your Anxiety and Panic Records. Notice all the ways you are breaking your anxiety cycle. You may also keep working to reduce your triggers.

Chapter Summary

In this chapter you have learned why it is important to face your fears and teach your Reacting Brain that anxiety sensations are safe. You have also done physical exercises that create the same physical sensations as panic and learned how to repeat these exercises until they no longer frighten you.

Track your progress using Form 12-99 Completed Chapter 12. Note things you have learned, or been surprised by, in this chapter.

This completes Step 5. Check Form 1-03: Reward Plan (page 16) to see if you planned a reward for completing this step. .

Form 12-99: Completed Chapter 12

Date completed: _____

Lessons learned:

_____

Example: Raj's Physical Exercise Subsequent Practice 1

```
0-----1------2------3------4------5------6------7------8------9-------10
None       Mild           Medium        Strong         Worst
```

Date	Physical Exercise	Practice 0-5	Anxiety 0-10	What are you learning
8/11	Muscle Tensing	1	4	
8/11	Muscle Tensing	2	3	
8/11	Muscle Tensing	3	3	
8/11	Muscle Tensing	4	2	
8/11	Muscle Tensing	5	1	Tense muscles are not the same as being out of control
8/12	Straw Breathing	1	4	
8/12	Straw Breathing	2	3	
8/12	Straw Breathing	3	2	I start out scared it lessens with practice
8/12	Straw Breathing	4	2	
8/12	Straw Breathing	5	1	
8/13	Balloon Breathing	1	5	
8/13	Balloon Breathing	2	5	
8/13	Balloon Breathing	3	4	
8/13	Balloon Breathing	4	4	
8/13	Balloon Breathing	5	4	I need to keep practicing and remind myself of the facts.

Example: Raj's Physical Exercise Subsequent Practice 2

```
0-----1------2------3------4------5------6------7------8------9-------10
None        Mild            Medium          Strong          Worst
```

Date	Physical Exercise	Practice 0-5	Anxiety 0-10	What are you learning
8/14	Balloon Breathing	1	4	
8/14	Balloon Breathing	2	3	
8/14	Balloon Breathing	3	3	The feelings don't have to scare me.
8/14	Balloon Breathing	4	2	
8/14	Balloon Breathing	5	1	Weird, strong feelings but no fear or danger
8/15	Head Lift	1	5	
8/15	Head Lift	2	3	
8/15	Head Lift	3	1	That went down really fast. This works!

Example: Carlos' Physical Exercise Subsequent Practice 1

```
0-----1------2------3------4------5------6------7------8------9-------10
None        Mild           Medium         Strong          Worst
```

Date	Physical Exercise	Practice 0-5	Anxiety 0-10	What are you learning
9/15	Staring at Wall	1	2	
9/15	Staring at Wall	2	1	
9/15	Staring at Wall	3	0	I don't have to worry about this
9/15	Spinning	1	3	
9/15	Spinning	2	3	
9/15	Spinning	3	2	
9/15	Spinning	4	1	Feelings can be safe
9/15	Spinning	5	0	Dizzy doesn't mean something's wrong
9/16	Straw Breathing	1	4	
9/16	Straw Breathing	2	4	
9/16	Straw Breathing	3	3	
9/16	Straw Breathing	4	3	
9/16	Straw Breathing	5	2	It gets better the more I do it

Example: Carlos' Physical Exercise Subsequent Practice 2

```
0-----1------2------3------4------5------6------7------8------9-------10
None         Mild          Medium          Strong          Worst
```

Date	Physical Exercise	Practice 0-5	Anxiety 0-10	What are you learning
9/17	Straw Breathing	1	2	
9/17	Straw Breathing	2	1	
9/17	Muscle Tensing	1	5	
9/17	Muscle Tensing	2	5	
9/17	Muscle Tensing	3	4	
9/17	Muscle Tensing	4	4	
9/17	Muscle Tensing	5	3	I'm worrying less about my body & my health
9/18	Muscle Tensing	1	4	
9/18	Muscle Tensing	2	3	
9/18	Muscle Tensing	3	3	
9/18	Muscle Tensing	4	2	
9/18	Muscle Tensing	5	1	

Chapter **13**:
Step 6 Learn Activities Are Safe

"For the first month after I started having panic attacks, I didn't leave the house. And then I thought, 'If I'm going to get any better, I have to go out.' So I told my friends, 'Please don't let me back out of things' and I started going places again." — Amy

If you have completed your subsequent practice exercises and none of them scare you anymore, congratulations! If you are partway through your list, that's great! Continue subsequent practice until you finish your list of exercises. You can move ahead while continuing your exercises or complete your exercises before moving on.

Look at your progress so far. What has practice taught you about how facing fears reduces them? What patterns and changes are you noticing in your Anxiety and Panic Records? How are you breaking your anxiety cycle?

If you have *not* done the subsequent practice (or have skipped other earlier steps), you are welcome to keep going. However, I do encourage you to do the forms and exercises at some point. The Fears vs. Facts form in Chapter 11 and the exercises in Chapter 12 are particularly powerful and important tools for overcoming anxiety and panic. Using them will help you get the best and most long-lasting results.

Teach Your Reacting Brain Feared Activities Are Safe

If you still fear or avoid certain activities or situations, this chapter will help you convince your Reacting Brain that these activities and situations are safe. You are very, very close to freedom.

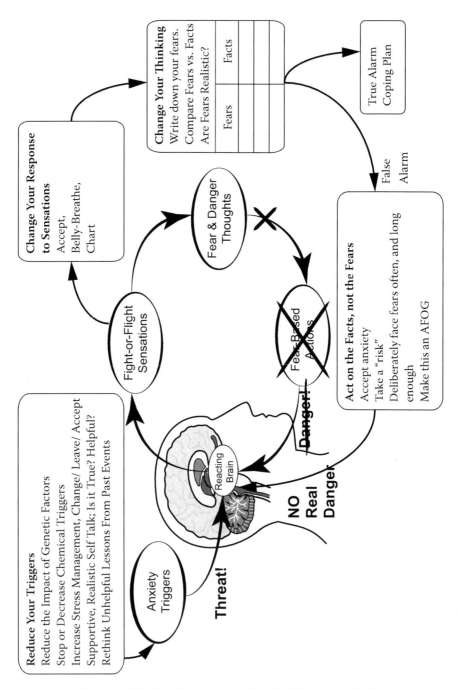

Figure 13-01: Learning Activities Are Safe

Words program your brain to some extent, but actions are even more powerful, especially for retraining your Reacting Brain. Combine the power of both by **acting** on your new true and helpful, **fact-based thinking**.

You must **show** your Reacting Brain that situations it thinks threaten you are *not dangerous*. And because **it learns through experience**, deliberately facing your feared activities is essential. When your *fears* say one thing and the *facts* say another, follow this rule:

Act on the Facts, Not the Fear.

Remember, you would not let a two-year-old drive your car. Do not let your child-like Reacting Brain drive your life! The results will not be pretty.

Be a loving–but firm–parent to your child-like brain. Do what is best in the long run–even if your Reacting Brain gets scared temporarily and has a temper tantrum.

Create Your Activities/Situations Practice Plan

Form 13-01 includes activities and situations that many people with anxiety or panic find frightening or avoid. Make this into your personal practice plan by adding your specific activities or situations in the spaces provided.

Think about how fear of panic or anxiety has been affecting or limiting your activities. As you read the list, think about whether each activity or situation makes you feel anxious, or fearful and hypervigilant.

Use Form 13-01: Activities and Situations List (page 235) to create your personal practice plan.

Rate each activity or situation on this list using this 0-4 scale:

0. Do without fear or Not Applicable. Some situations—like disagreeing or driving in heavy traffic—may cause stress, but they do not scare you, cause fear, or trigger panic.

1. Fear but do anyway. If the activity or situation makes you anxious but you still do it.

2. Do but in a 'Safe Way.' If you do this activity but only in a special way with some "safety action."

3. Do but leave if feel panic. If you leave when you start to feel panicky or anxious.

4. Avoid or do not do at all. If you completely avoid the activity or situation out of fear.

At the bottom of the form, add any other activities and situations you fear or avoid that are not already on the list. Then rate each added activity or situation.

Compare this form with your Form 8-03: Panic Records (page 114) and Form 7-01: Fear-Based Actions Checklist (page 96) to make sure you have included everything that is important to you. Don't let fear or panic continue to restrict your life!

Form 13-01: Activities and Situations List

Rate each activity or situation on the next page using this 0-4 scale:

0. Do without fear or Not Applicable

1. Fear but do anyway

2. Do but in a 'Safe Way'

3. Do but leave if feel panic

4. Avoid or don't do at all

Breaking the Final Link in Your Anxiety Cycle

Good work. Your Activities and Situations form tells you *specifically* which activities and situations your caveman Reacting Brain needs to learn are safe. Using this list, you can convince your protective, bodyguard brain that there is, in fact, no life-threatening danger in these situations <u>and</u> that you can cope. Each activity is a steppingstone on your path to freedom.

Activities and Situations Practice

Schedule time to deliberately practice each activity or situation on your list that you rated 2 or higher. Practice each activity and situation on your list as often as possible.

If you worry that practice might be dangerous, review Chapter 11: Change Your Thinking, especially the part about Fears vs. Facts. Use your smart rational Thinking Brain to decide how much danger each activity really poses,

Form 13-01: Activities and Situations List

Activities and Situations	Rating 0-4
Leave home	
Go far from home or somewhere unfamiliar	
Go places alone	
Be a passenger in a car	
Drive alone, with people, or with children in the car	
Drive on the freeway	
Drive in lots of traffic or in a traffic jam	
Drive on bridges, overpasses, tunnels, or other roadways	
Go to large stores, malls, movies, fairs, or other places with crowds or lines	
Go on a long airplane flight	
Take the bus, subway, or train	
Go places you can't easily leave like the doctor, dentist, backseat of a car, middle of a row, auditorium, theater, stadium or concert hall	
Go places without a nearby bathroom	
Take escalators or crowded elevators	
Go to work or school	
Speak up in meetings or class	
Go to parties or social situations	
Be alone	
Do exciting things that bring on strong emotions like sports events, scary movies, sex, disagreeing or arguing	
Drink or eat something with caffeine (tea, coffee, chocolate)	
Be in small spaces or hot, stuffy spaces	
Heights, high floors of tall buildings	

how likely any danger is, and how you can cope. <u>Put your Thinking Brain in charge.</u>

Track your practice using Form 13-02: Activities and Situations Practice Record:

Use one line on the Activities and Situations Practice Record for each practice. Record the date and what you did in the notes area.

Tackle the items on your Activities and Situations List in any order. You may want to focus on changing one activity or situation at a time, or you may want to change as many as possible. Your goal is to have ratings of 0 or 1 for all your activities and situations.

When you can do an activity or face a situation without distressing fear, without "safety actions," and without leaving if you feel panicky (Rating of 0 or 1), cross it off your Activities and Situations List.

Form 13-02: Activities and Situations Practice Record

Rate each activity or situation on the next page using this 0-4 scale:

0. Do without fear or Not Applicable

1. Fear but do anyway

2. Do but in a 'Safe Way'

3. Do but leave if feel panic

4. Avoid or don't do at all

The more situations you face, the more positive changes occur. Your Thinking Brain becomes stronger and more in charge. Your Reacting Brain becomes more reassured and calmer.

Each time you deliberately face a feared situation without leaving or "safety actions," you weaken the panic cycle and strengthen the positive cycle of knowledge, confidence, and skill. Think about how wonderful that is for your life. Let the excitement of that outweigh and counterbalance any anticipatory anxiety or temporary fear.

Form 13-02: Activities and Situations Practice Record

Activity or Situation	Rating 0-4	Notes

Think about where you were when you started this book and the progress you have made. Where are you now? Where do you want to be? Activities and Situations Practice will help you reach your goal.

Activities/Situations Practice Rules

Every time you face an activity or situation on your practice list, you take a step closer to your goal. It is just like walking along a path to get somewhere or climbing the steps of a staircase to reach the top. And, just like on a path or a stairway, you can take *many small* steps, or *a few giant* steps.

When you take small steps, each step is easier, but you have to take more steps and it may take a bit longer. If you take big, giant steps, each step is more work, but you reach your goal more quickly.

Face your fears in small or large steps. Both approaches work. The choice is up to you.

I encourage you to:

1. Take the biggest "step" toward your goal that you can, but also

2. Make each "step" as small as you need in order to actually take the step and face the feared activity or situation.

Find the right balance of "big" and "small" steps toward your goal. Keep going until you break your anxiety cycle and are free.

Activities/Situations Practice Motto

"As big as you can.

As small as you need.

Keep taking those steps

Until you are freed."

Can I be sure this is safe?

If you worry about an activity or situation on your practice list, review the facts about it. Ask yourself: "Do other people do these activities and enter these situations without anxiety or special precautions?"

Remember, you are *not* seeking an absolute guarantee of total safety or total certainty. We do not get guarantees like this in life. No one does.

If you let your anxiety sucker you into demanding guaranteed total safety, I can promise you one thing: you *are* guaranteed to get *more worry, uncertainty, and anxiety*! Do not seek perfect guarantees. Act on the facts. Act on the odds. Act the way people who don't have panic act.

Recognizing that a bad outcome is *possible* is **not** the same thing as thinking that outcome is *likely*. It is *possible* that you could be killed by a meteor crashing into your home, office, clinic, coffee shop, or wherever you are reading this. However, this event is highly unlikely, and I imagine that you do not spend a lot of time worrying about meteor strikes or changing your behavior due to a fear of meteors.

This is the attitude and the approach you want to take toward other unrealistic, unlikely fears. Treat them like meteors!

Think About What You Will Gain

You started reading this book because anxiety and panic were causing you distress and interfering with your happiness. Imagine the relief and benefits of truly being free–of no longer letting fear of panic restrict your life.

Think how much your life has improved–or will improve–as you help your caveman Reacting Brain leap into action *only when appropriate*. Life will be much happier and more relaxed. You no longer unthinkingly respond when your Reacting Brain misfires or overestimates dangers, instead you will use and listen to the Thinking Brain.

You may have already noticed improvements in your life. Completing Step 6 in the program builds upon and strengthens those improvements.

Of all the steps in this program, Step 6 is the most powerful. Fear-based actions—such as taking "safety actions," looking for danger, leaving, avoiding, or fighting the anxiety response out of fear—maintain and strengthen the vicious cycle of anxiety and panic. Stopping these actions breaks that cycle and truly frees you.

Story: Raj

By this point, Raj was a lot less anxious, but a few activities still made him nervous. He continued to avoid some situations or leave if he felt panic sensations or anxiety. After completing his Activities and Situations form, he told us, "I know it is time to face these if I want a normal life again." He began deliberately and repeatedly facing the activities and situations on his list.

Two Approaches That Work–and One That Doesn't

"You can't cross a sea by merely staring into the water."
–Rabindranath Tagore

You *must face* your feared activities and situations. Your Reacting Brain must see for itself that the "threat" from these activities and situations is not as bad as it fears. Two approaches work.

Approach One: Jump in. This works!

You "jump in the deep end" and get it over with all at once. You keep reminding yourself that these activities are not dangerous (just scary) and that the way to get over them being scary is to do them—remembering that they are not dangerous.

You confront your most feared situations as soon as possible, as often as possible, and for as long as possible. You go out of your way to do all your feared activities, especially the scariest ones, and you stay in each situation until you (and your Reacting Brain) become bored.

Having faced your worst fears, it is awfully hard to be frightened of lesser fears. This is the "take a few big steps" approach.

Approach One works. It feels scariest, but gives the fastest results.

Story: Raj

After Raj understood what was happening with his Reacting Brain, he decided to jump in and face his most feared situations. He went out of his way to attend work luncheons and other social activities that involved food. He invited his friends and family to go out and eat with him, and he made

Example: Raj's Activities and Situations Form

Activities and Situations	Rating 0-4
Leave home	0
Go far from home or somewhere unfamiliar	1
Go places alone	0
Be a passenger in a car	0
Drive alone, with people, or with children in the car	0
Drive on the freeway	0
Drive in lots of traffic or in a traffic jam	0
Drive on bridges, overpasses, tunnels, or other roadways	0
Go to large stores, malls, movies, fairs, or other places with crowds or lines	2
Go on a long airplane flight	2
Take the bus, subway, or train	0
Go places you can't easily leave like the doctor, dentist, backseat of a car, middle of a row, auditorium, theater, stadium or concert hall	3
Go places without a nearby bathroom	4
Take escalators or crowded elevators	0
Go to work or school	2
Speak up in meetings or class	0
Go to parties or social situations	4
Be alone	0
Do exciting things that bring on strong emotions like sports events, scary movies, sex, disagreeing or arguing	0
Drink or eat something with caffeine (tea, coffee, chocolate)	0
Be in small spaces or hot, stuffy spaces	2
Heights, high floors of tall buildings	0
Eating in public	3
Eating with friends	3
Eating with coworkers	4

Figure 13-02: You can take big steps

a point to eat as he normally would (i.e. resisting the temptation to eat only small bites, etc.). At first, Raj was quite nervous and panicky. You can imagine how scary this was for him! But he kept using his belly breathing and telling himself, "Act on the facts, not the fears."

Raj later told us, "Eating with coworkers and my boss was the hardest! But I was tired of anxiety controlling my life. I just said to myself, 'If I throw up, I throw up. Just do it and be done with it!' Oddly enough, I almost immediately stopped being nauseous! I can't believe it. I feel so much better."

Approach Two: Many Small Steps. This works!

You "dip a toe in the water and enter the pool gradually" with this approach. You begin with the least scary activities and work up to the scariest. This is the "take many small steps" approach.

Figure 13-03: Or many smaller steps

Do *not* stop halfway through your list thinking you have made "good enough" progress. Keep going all the way to the end of your list, until you have changed all your fear actions and faced all your fears.

Halfway overcoming fear leaves you vulnerable and makes fear more likely to return. Doing this is like taking half a dose of antibiotics: the symptoms have improved, but the infection is still there and is likely to flare up again. Or like leaving campfire only partly put out; it is no longer burning, but the hot coals can catch fire again. You want the infection completely wiped out; you want the fire completely doused. You want to leave no toehold for anxiety or panic to sneak back into your life.

Approach Two works. It feels less scary, but it takes longer. As long as you complete your entire list, it does work.

Story: Amanda

Amanda used a "baby steps" approach to overcoming her fear of the mall. She began by driving past the mall, without stopping. Next, she drove into the parking lot and forced herself to stay until her anxiety went down.

After that no longer scared her, she parked, got out of her car, and sat by the mall entrance without going in. This took several practices, but each time she stayed until her anxiety level went down.

Her next step was going into the mall. This took courage. At times, she doubted she could do it, but she kept reminding herself of the facts. She made a list of all the fears and facts, carried it with her, and read it over and over while facing her fears. She also used low-and-slow belly breathing.

Despite her fear, Amanda eventually entered the mall and walked all the way to the middle! She stayed there until her anxiety level went down. Eventually she was able to spend two hours in the mall and actually shop without anxiety.

This approach took longer than jumping into the worst fear, but it was the best approach for Amanda. As she said, "It worked!"

Approach Three: This Does NOT Work!

You postpone. You find excuses. You decide to wait until you don't have any fear. You only face situations when forced to and you leave as soon as possible and/or take "safety" actions.

With this approach, you let your anxiety talk you out of practicing altogether. Or if you *do* practice, you practice as little and as briefly as possible, white-knuckling it through and hoping you never have to do it again.

In other words, you pretty much let your overly fearful, primitive, child-like caveman Reacting Brain decide if, when, and how you practice. But if your Reacting Brain was such a terrific guide, you wouldn't be here in the first place, right?

So, reread all the facts about panic and your fears. Grab your courage in both hands. And put *you* and your *Thinking* Brain in charge.

Figure 13-04: Wishing and hoping will not get you there!

Your caveman Reacting Brain thinks it's helping you, but *it* needs help. Take charge with your Thinking Brain. Don't let your Reacting Brain drive the car of your life into a ditch. Take the wheel. Push your caveman brain into the passenger seat or—even better—strap it into a car seat in back.

Practice Pointers

Keep Taking the Next Step

Make each step *as big as you can*—and *as small as you need*. It does not matter how many steps there are between you and your goal.

What *does matter* is taking the next step, whatever that is. Just take the next step. Do not stop.

Let Fear Be Your Guide—Do the Opposite!

Transform feelings of fear, anxiety, worry, or panic into helpful guides. These feelings are proof that your Reacting Brain needs to learn something.

Use these feelings:

- If fear tells you to *do* something, do *the opposite.*

- If fear tells you *not* to do something, go ahead and *do it*— as soon as possible and repeatedly.

Trust the Process

Trust the learning process and give it time to show success. You may be scared or uncertain but keep taking steps towards your goal.

In some ways, the process of change is like the process of planting flowers in a garden. You plant a seed and do things to help it grow. You *keep doing these things for a while before you see growth and results.*

You give it time. You keep up your efforts and trust that your work will pay off. You don't dig a seedling up every day to see if it is growing. It needs time. The same is true for this approach.

Be willing to trust the process. Over time, often much less time than you expect, your actions will result in clear, obvious changes. By following these steps, you can overcome your fear of panic. Your life can open up and bloom in wonderful ways.

Starting This Week

Find or create opportunities to face all the activities and situations on your list until none of them scare you.

If any of the physical exercises still cause you anxiety, practice those ones until they no longer scare you.

Work on any part of your personal anxiety cycle that still needs to be addressed. See the next chapter for help with specific issues.

Continue keeping Anxiety Records and Panic Records to track your progress until you have broken out of your anxiety cycle and panic no longer affects your life.

Chapter Summary

In this chapter you have learned that activities and situations—that you previously feared—are safe by repeatedly facing these situations until your Reacting Brain finally gets the message. We have also covered practical pointers to help you through this process.

Track your progress using Form 13-99: Completed Chapter 13. Note things you have learned, or been surprised by, in this chapter.

Congratulations, this completes Step 6, the final step in this process. Check Form 1-03: Reward Plan (page 16) and see if you planned to reward yourself for completing this step.

Form 13-99: Completed Chapter 13

Date completed: _____

Lessons learned:

_____

Chapter 14

Problems and Solutions

"Obstacles don't have to stop you. If you run into a wall, don't turn around and give up. Figure out how to climb it, go through it, or work around it." — Michael Jordan

This chapter covers issues some people encounter while learning to overcome anxiety and panic. These topics include:

- What to do if you take anti-anxiety medicine,

- Fear situations that can't be faced in reality,

- Frightening memories,

- Dealing with reality-based uncertainty,

- Continuing to have panic attacks despite facing feared activities,

- Feeling too scared to change your actions, or

- Not being able to make changes. despite wanting to change.

Select and read any sections that apply to you. If none of these topics apply, skip to the next chapter.

I Take Anti-Anxiety Medicine

For the reasons discussed earlier (see Do I need anti-anxiety medication on page 34), I believe that most people who have anxiety or panic get the best results by applying the skills taught in this book without using anti-anxiety medicine.

If you currently take anti-anxiety medication, please *continue* taking your medication as prescribed until you get new instructions from the healthcare provider who prescribed the medication. Work with your healthcare team to coordinate any medication changes with the process of learning to overcome anxiety and panic. If there is a change in your medication, follow the new instructions carefully as the dose may be reduced gradually.

Short-acting anti-anxiety medicines can interfere with this treatment in all of the following ways:

- Chemical effects of short-acting anti-anxiety medications can interfere with learning and memory.

- If the medicine prevents you from feeling anxiety or panic sensations, you do not have a chance to learn that the sensations are harmless.

Using medicine to prevent or stop panic is avoiding and/or fighting the natural anxiety response. These are fear-based actions that can strengthen the anxiety cycle and make it very hard for your bodyguard Reacting Brain to believe that you would have been safe without the medicine. It may think you only survived or coped because you took medicine.

However, some people find that medication helps them to start practicing these skills, and that after practicing *with* medication, they then have the courage to practice *without* medication. As my former colleague Stephen Chen, PsyD, explains it:

> "Short-acting anti-anxiety medicines such as Xanax (Alprazolam), Ativan (Lorazepam), Klonopin (Clonazepam), etc. are like training wheels that help you learn to ride a bicycle. They give you the courage to start riding which helps you develop your bike-riding skills. But, after practicing with training wheels, you need to take them off and ride without them—even if you're a little scared at first. Training wheels are temporary."

If you are taking medicine to prevent panic attacks, consider asking your healthcare provider about stopping the medication. Reread the information on Do I Need Anti-Anxiety Medicine? (page 34) to understand why I suggest this.

If anti-anxiety medication was prescribed solely to stop panic attacks, the person prescribing the medicine may recommend that you reduce the dosage and stop the medicine while you learn and practice the skills in this book.

There are several reasons for this common recommendation:

- You will learn other skills. These may replace the medicine.

- As you lose your fear of anxiety sensations, you have less need for medicine to stop or prevent these sensations.

- Panic attacks will become less frequent, shorter, and less severe as you understand panic, change your thinking, and face your fears.

- These experiences show your Reacting Brain that you do not need medicine to "protect" you from the unpleasant – but harmless – sensations.

How do I stop the medicine if I want to?

Talk to the medical professional who prescribed your medication before making any change in how you take any medicine. This can be particularly important for anti-anxiety medications.

If you take anti-anxiety medication every day, your healthcare provider will probably want you to reduce the medicine gradually, especially if you have been regularly taking fast-acting anti-anxiety medications such as Xanax (Alprazolam), Ativan (Lorazepam), Klonopin (Clonazepam), and others. These medicines can be physically (and emotionally) addicting and can cause serious (or even fatal) problems if you suddenly stop, especially if you have been taking large doses over a long period.

If you are taking this type of medicine, **do not suddenly stop it without speaking to your healthcare provide**r. Get medical advice on how to decrease and stop safely.

My Feared Activity Can't be Faced in Reality

Some activities are difficult or impossible to practice facing in reality. They may be expensive, like airplane flights, or require too much time, like taking long road trips. Other feared activities can't be faced now because they will happen in the future, like going on a cruise, giving a talk in public, going through medical treatment, etc. Other activities happened in the past and you can't travel back in time. Here are some solutions.

Use your imagination

Imagine doing the activities. This works because your Reacting Brain cannot tell the difference between what is real and what is not.

First, imagine that you are doing the activity. Write down every detail as if you were going through it right this moment. Write everything you expect you will do, feel, think, and say. Be sure to write it in the present tense ("I am...", "I do...", "I feel...", "I think...", I tell myself...", "I say...").

Write down how you will cope *successfully* and overcome any fears. End your writing describing how you successfully completed the activity despite anxiety or panic. The goal is *not* to avoid experiencing anxiety or fear; the goal is to successfully handle anxiety or panic without leaving or resorting to "safety actions."

Now read what you have written over and over again, imagining that it is really happening. Notice how your anxiety drops over time with repetition. You are practicing deliberately facing the situation successfully.

If writing is a problem for you, make a voice recording following the instructions above. Listen to the recording over and over.

Find a therapist offering virtual reality therapy

Virtual reality therapy (VRT), also known as virtual reality exposure therapy (VRET), is becoming more widely available. I have been using VRT with clients since 2010, along with the tools taught in this book. My clients have found this combination to be exceptionally helpful in overcoming anxiety, panic, fears, and phobias.

Virtual reality (VR) technology creates the experience of being inside an immersive, 3-dimensional computer-generated environment where you can "face your fears" gradually while your therapist guides and monitors you. You see and hear a realistic simulation (or a 3-dimensional video) that can be controlled by your therapist and tailored to be helpful for you.

For example, if being on an airplane makes you panic, instead of having to imagine flying, you can put on a VR headset and "fly" in a virtual plane. Flying in virtual reality lets you practice using your anxiety coping skills and helps you work up to flying in real life. VR bridges the gap between the therapy office and reality.

Virtual reality lets you face fears *in* the therapist's office while your therapist coaches and supports you. With VR, you can face feared activities like flying that would be expensive and time-consuming to repeatedly practice in real life. In VR, you can go on as many flights as you need until you overcome your fear. If the process of takeoff makes you anxious, on a virtual plane, you can take off as many times as you like—not something you can ask the pilot to do in real life!

More than thirty different virtual environments (VEs) are available to help overcome fears and more are being developed all the time. There are VEs for fears of flying, driving, public speaking, heights, needles, spiders, tests, claustrophobia, darkness, elevators, public transportation, open spaces, storms, and many other situations in which people sometimes panic.

Some Veterans' Administration facilities offer virtual reality therapy for soldiers with war-related post-traumatic stress disorder (PTSD). Specialized VEs have been developed to help with the aftermath of sexual assault.

For more information on finding a therapist see the Appendix.

I Have Memories That Scare Me

The writing approach described above for reducing past event triggers can also be used for facing scary memories. By *deliberately and repeatedly* confronting a past experience in a controlled way, you can change *both* your *physical and emotional response* to the memory *and* the way you *think* about what happened.

Reducing Past Event Triggers (page 136) describes how to use this approach to relive and rethink memories of past panic attacks. You can use the same approach to help with other frightening memories as well, such as recalling nightmares, scary movies, or upsetting events.

However, if you plan to write about a traumatic event such as being raped, molested, abused, assaulted, almost dying, seeing someone die, being in a war, or something similarly severe, consult a mental health professional before using this technique on your own. Ask if this writing exercise is appropriate for you. Arrange for professional help if you think you may need it, or if you have signs of post-traumatic stress disorder (see page 57).

I am Dealing with Uncertainty

As discussed earlier, when fears are supported by the facts, your Reacting Brain is sending a true alarm. Uncertainty is when you *do* face a reality-based likely threat, but do *not* know how serious the threat may be.

Uncertainty tends to make anxious worry more intense and, of course, can trigger panic. You don't know exactly what will happen. You don't know when or how bad the problem will be. You don't know what you will need to do.

People really dislike uncertainty, so a common response is to try to figure out what will happen. The problem is that you cannot know the future, so your view of the future will be based not only on the facts you have, but also on *what you tell yourself.*

When you face uncertainty, you typically are asking three questions:

- "What will happen? What is possible and how bad might it be?"
- "When will it happen? How near or distant is the threat?"
- "What can I do? What are my options now and in the future?"

Look at All the Likely Options and Outcomes

Fear thoughts can leap to the worst conclusion, vividly predicting a terrible outcome. This can be so scary and convincing you forget that your Reacting Brain *does not know* the future. Take for example, the fear thought, "I have a lump in my breast. I'm going to die soon of cancer!"

Finding a breast lump is certainly a potential threat and needs to be investigated. This is a reality-based fear and you should take appropriate action.

At the same time, the fact of a breast lump does *not* prove you have cancer or will die soon.

In reality, there are a series of questions to be considered, such as: Does the mammogram show that the lump is a tumor–or not? *If* it is a tumor, what type and stage tumor is it? What are the treatment options? What is the outlook (prognosis) following each type of treatment? Treatments and outcomes differ. People differ.

Similarly, if your children are making bad choices, you may worry about them. If your employer announces layoffs or your manager seems to dislike you, you may worry about your job security. Potential threats can have some basis in reality. At the same time, there has *always* been uncertainty in life and there *will* always be uncertainty in life. You can always find things about which to worry.

So slow down. Iinstead of imagining the worst feared outcome, think logically through *each of the possible options*. Take it one step at a time. Don't let fear leap over the process of gathering information and thinking through options. Help your Thinking Brain identify *all* the potential outcomes. Get information from experts and/or people who have faced similar situations.

Your emotional response to situations of risk and uncertainty is affected partly by facts, but also by what you tell yourself. Whenever possible, you want to foster hope. Remember that you want your self-talk to be not only true, but *helpful*. Assuming the worst and giving up hope is not helpful.

Since you *cannot* know the future, plan for the worst but *hope for the best*. When you deal with uncertainty, take reasonable steps, then focus on the possible *good* outcomes. Deliberately create optimism and hope because they, in turn, foster happiness, effective problem-solving, and perseverance.

I Confront Feared Activities, but Panic Attacks Continue!

Sometimes panic attacks continue, even after you face feared activities or situations, because it takes time for your primitive caveman Reacting Brain to learn that you are safe. Be patient with it. After all, it is designed to learn and remember danger—not safety. Sometimes you just need a little more practice.

Taking anti-anxiety medicine while facing your fears may slow the learning process. Reread the section on I Take Anti-Anxiety Medicine (page 247).

Consider whether you may be practicing in a way that is not effective or if there are other issues. If you have been facing your fears but still have panic attacks, ask yourself these questions.

Am I taking "safety actions"?

Safety actions are things you do that make you feel "safe" *when you are not really in danger.* These can be mental thoughts, images, distractions, reassuring yourself, or physical activities like choosing where you are, who you are with, carrying something with you, opening the windows, blowing cool air, etc.

Either the facts say you are in danger, these actions are *truly* protective, and *everyone* agrees and does them—or the facts say you are *not in danger*, these actions do *nothing* to keep you safe, and other people *don't* do them. What do the facts say?

When the facts say this is a false alarm, *stop* all safety actions as soon as possible. When you take unneeded "safety actions," your Reacting Brain believes you only survived because of these actions and remains convinced that the situation you faced really is dangerous (because otherwise why would you take a safety action). It will continue to send false alarms.

If you are going to the effort of facing your fear, I encourage you, as soon as possible, to do it in the most effective way. You want your efforts to pay off.

Do I mentally avoid or escape?

Avoiding or escaping by using distraction, imagery, or other techniques can blunt the effectiveness of these exercises. Remember, basically you need to drag your caveman Reacting Brain into a situation it thinks is dangerous, force it to *pay attention,* and stay there long enough to calm down, so it eventually learns that you are okay.

If you are not paying attention and focusing, your Reacting Brain will not learn the lesson of safety.

Is my problem real? If so, do I have a plan and am I following it?

If your anxiety is sounding a true alarm about a real-life problem, you must cope with that problem. If you are *not* taking steps to solve or cope with the problem, your Reacting Brain will keep bugging you until you *do* take care of it. After all, that is its job! See Responding to a True Alarm (page 180) for information on making and following a plan.

Are my triggers being hit?

Reread Chapter 3: Your Anxiety Triggers and review your Form 8-03: Panic Records (page 114) to make sure you have identified all of your triggers. Look at your life. What can you do to decrease your triggers?

- Stop any chemicals that might trigger panic (see page 125) and see how you feel.

- Check with your healthcare provider if you think your anxiety or panic symptoms could be caused by a medical condition or by medication.

- Improve your stress management, see page 127.

- Improve your negative self-talk and self-demands, see Form 3-04: Negative Self-Talk Checklist (page 51) and Form 3-05: Unrealistic Self-Demands Checklist (page 52).

Your Reacting Brain may be trying to get you to take action to reduce a trigger, or change some other part of the panic cycle. Panic can be an AFOG. Perhaps this is Another F_____ (fantastic, fabulous, f---ing) Opportunity for Growth. Look at the bigger picture. Think and act in ways that weaken your panic cycle and improve your life.

Do I have a problem other than panic attacks?

Sometimes panic can be caused by, or accompanied by, other issues. For example, specific fears or phobias, social anxiety, post-traumatic stress disorder (PTSD), obsessive-compulsive disorder (OCD), generalized anxiety disorder (GAD), depression, etc.

If you think you may have additional issues, especially if you are doing everything I suggest and not improving, consult a licensed mental health professional (see the Appendix). Ask if panic is the only, or primary, issue you should treat or whether there are other issues.

I am Too Scared to Change My Actions

*"I was so scared. I didn't want to go anywhere or do anything. My
husband and my mother had to really encourage me. I finally realized I
<u>had</u> to change for the sake of my children." – Elizabeth*

If you *want* to change your actions but are too frightened, examine what
frightens you in more detail. Which fear thoughts keep you from taking the
recommended actions? Review the anxiety cycle (Chapter 2: The Anxiety
Cycle). Use the questions below to select your next step.

Do I not understand panic? Does it still seem dangerous?

If you do not understand what happens during a panic attack, or if anxiety
still scares you, reread Chapter 2: The Anxiety Cycle and learn more about
panic and anxiety. Understand all the parts of your personal anxiety cycle in
Chapters 3 to 9, being sure to complete *all* the forms and exercises.

Do I need to reduce my triggers?

Make sure you have identified *all* your triggers by reviewing your forms in
Chapter 3 Your Anxiety Triggers and your Form 8-03: Panic Records (page
114).

If you need to further reduce your anxiety triggers, review Chapter 9: Reduce Your Triggers and follow the suggestions for reducing triggers. *Do not*
use this as an excuse to avoid overcoming your fear of anxiety. You can do all
the other steps before or while reducing triggers.

Am I having problems with belly breathing?

Belly breathing can help you tolerate anxiety, which lets you face your fears.
It also helps to calm many anxiety symptoms.

If you are having trouble starting belly breathing when you are anxious, or
if you belly breathe rapidly, you may be chronically hyperventilating. Reread
the instructions for Belly Breathing (page 147). During a time when you
not feeling anxious, practice belly breathing while counting and breathing
low-and-slow.

Practice deliberately shifting to belly breathing multiple times throughout the day. As you become skilled at changing your breathing quickly and easily, you will be more able to use belly breathing even when you feel anxious or panicky.

Breathe2Relax is a free app for Android and iPhone that many people have found to be helpful in learning belly breathing.

If you have trouble learning to do belly breathing, or find that belly breathing is not helping you, focus on using other skills.

Have I identified and put all my fears into words?

Does your Reacting Brain worry about fears, threats, or risks that you have not yet identified and put into words? Reread Chapter 3: Your Personal Anxiety Cycle and Chapter 6: Your Fear and Danger Thoughts. Figure out what *specifically* your Reacting Brain fears, so you can evaluate whether these fears are realistic.

Begin with these steps:

- Review your forms, especially your Form 8-03: Panic Records (page 114) to identify fears.

- Start filling out a Form 8-03: Panic Record for every little surge of anxiety you experience.

- Relive your past panic attacks and fill out Panic Records for them.

- Write down all the fears, worries, anxieties, and/or distressing, upsetting, or scary thoughts that flash through your mind when you get anxious, fearful, or panicky.

- Use your imagination to think up the worst possible outcomes of panic.

Have I analyzed all my fears?

Ask questions like "What am I afraid might happen if I felt that sensation or confronted my feared activities? What is my worst-case nightmare feared outcome?" Imagine these scenarios all the way through to the end.

Keep asking questions: "And if I did that or felt that or that thing happened, what might happen next? What might that mean about me, or my future, or other people? And then what? And then what?" and so on.

Answer the questions, even if you have to guess. Put the answers, the predictions, and the unvoiced underlying assumptions into words. Get very specific and detailed.

Coax your Reacting Brain into revealing all the horrible outcomes it fears. Make it show you the horror movie it plays inside your skull so you can compare that to actual reality. Maybe the zombie apocalypse isn't really happening!

Now use your Thinking Brain to decide whether these fears are realistic. Go back to Chapter 11: Change Your Thinking and use the Fears vs. Facts form to help you and your Thinking Brain analyze, question, and challenge what is scaring your more primitive Reacting Brain unnecessarily.

Am I missing some needed information or facts?

Reread Chapter 11: Change Your Thinking to review the facts and complete or update your Fear vs. Facts form. Ask questions that uncover facts. If you need more information, talk with people who are reliable sources of information and can give you any specific missing facts you need. Practice consistently talking to yourself and to your Reacting Brain in ways that are both true and helpful.

Am I using true and helpful thinking?

If you are having trouble replacing fears with facts and thinking in ways that are both true and helpful, reread Chapter 3: Your Personal Anxiety Cycle, Chapter 6: Your Fear and Danger Thoughts and Chapter 11: Change Your Thinking. Pay special attention to the facts about your fears. Review all your forms, especially your Form 11-01: Fears vs. Facts (page 172).

Have I done the physical exercises?

Physical exercises help your Reacting Brain learn through experience that anxiety or panic sensations are not dangerous. If you have not done them, read Chapter 12: Learn Sensations Are Safe and do the physical exercises. Remember what you now know about the anxiety cycle: avoiding maintains the cycle of anxiety, fear, and panic; facing fears weakens the cycle.

If you are *afraid* to do the exercises, review the information on anxiety and sensations in Section 1, especially Chapter 2: The Anxiety Cycle, Chapter 3:

Your Personal Anxiety Cycle, and Chapter 5: Your Anxiety or Panic Sensations as well as and the facts about anxiety in Chapter 10: Change Your Response to Sensations. If you are *still* afraid of doing the exercises, ask a friend to do them with you, or find a therapist or a treatment group that does them. See the Appendix for information on finding a therapist.

Can I make facing my fears easier?

You can make facing a feared activity or situation easier in several ways. Here are some possibilities to get you started:

- Face your fear for brief periods of time; if possible, do this several times a day or several times a week. Gradually face your fear for longer periods of time.

- Face your fear in smaller steps.

- Have a friend with you at first when you face your fears.

- Start by facing the activity or situation in ways that seem easier or less scary. Then face the activity or situation in ways that seem scarier. Think of other ways to confront the fear more gradually or more easily.

- Visualize the activity or situation in your imagination before confronting it in reality. Follow the instructions in Use your imagination (page 250) to describe the situation in words and mentally practice it repeatedly before facing it in real-life.

- Find a therapist who offers virtual reality therapy (VRT), also known as virtual reality exposure therapy (VRET). You can face your fears in small steps that are controlled by the therapist and repeatable.

I Want to Change, but....

Is panic not your top priority? Do you have a more important issue to address first? If so, deal with your top priority, then turn your energy and attention to overcoming panic and anxiety.

Or are you puzzled, or frustrated, because you want to get better, but are not following the recommendations, even though you know they would help? For example, do you *mean* to complete the forms, but somehow never get to them? Do you *plan* to practice exercises or change actions, but never do?

You may have mixed feelings about making a change—even a desired change. You may not feel quite ready. You may have doubts about whether you can change or whether changing will be worthwhile. If this is the case, try the following ideas and see what happens.

Write and Reflect

Ask yourself the following questions in the order presented. Write down and reflect upon your answers:

1. "What will my life be like a year or five years if I _do not change_? Is this how I want to live my life?"

2. "How _could_ my life be different over the next one to five years if I follow these instructions and break my anxiety cycle? How can I _benefit_?"

3. What needs to be different for me to be ready, or willing, change? How can I make that happen?

4. What small steps am I willing to take _now_, even before anything else changes? One small step can lead to another.

Read Your Reasons to Change

You may have uncovered reasons to change when you completed your Form 11-01: Fear vs. Facts (page 172) form or during your Scheduled Daily Worry Time (see page 165).

Write down _which_ change(s) you want to make and _why_. Then read this list frequently. Add to it as more benefits of change occur to you.

Compare the _costs_ in time, energy, or money of making a change to the _benefits_ you will gain. Ask yourself what actions will make you feel better in the long run. If you are still not convinced, think and write about what may happen if you continue your current path _without making changes_.

Mentally Practice

Your brain and body react to what you imagine. Once you decide you _want_ to make a change, _mentally practice the change from start to finish_. Figure out the specific action steps to reach your goal. Then imagine yourself carrying out each step.

For example, if you decide to complete the forms, imagine how you will fill them out. Will you use your smartphone or your personal computer? Do you prefer paper forms? When and where will you work on these forms? Visualize yourself filling out the forms and praising yourself afterward. Step through how you will remind yourself to work on forms, and how you can make completing the forms as easy and simple as possible. Imagine every step of the process.

Use the same process for *any* change you want to make but have been postponing. Visualize the steps involved. You might imagine yourself reading this book, questioning your fears, doing the physical exercises, changing your actions, reducing anxiety triggers, or resolving a real-life problem.

If work stress is an anxiety trigger, imagine each step of finding a different job. Visualize yourself looking for jobs online and in the newspaper. See yourself updating your resume and completing job applications. Imagine going on interviews. Mentally rehearse how you will answer questions.

Similarly, if you have a real-life health problem, write down each action needed to heal it or cope with it. When will you call to make an appointment with your healthcare provider? What questions will you ask? How will you remember to take your medicine as prescribed? If you need to change what you eat or drink, how will you make those changes as easy as possible? What foods will you buy? And so on. Mentally rehearse carrying out each action.

Mental practice gets your mind and body ready. Don't visualize the end result; visualize the next few steps you will take.

And you don't have to change on your own. Find support.

Finding Support

Tell supportive friends and family about the specific changes you want to make. Tell them *what* you are going to change, *why* you are going to change, and *when* you are going to change. Ask them to support and encourage you. Tell them how they can help.

If you can find someone who wants to make similar changes, that's great. Having a "change buddy" can help you succeed.

Keep Track and Reward Yourself

You have decided *what* you want to change and *why*. You have, hopefully, found people who will support your changes. You know the steps to take and are visualizing yourself taking them. You are ready to take action.

Now track each of your steps along the path to change. You could make a "to do" list. You could schedule actions in your calendar and mark them "done". You could create a checklist like the ones in the book. Mark your progress.

Reward yourself for each little step. Rewards and praise keep you going. Celebrate alone, or with people who will praise you and support you.

Dealing with Setbacks

Maybe you skipped your exercise, meditation, yoga, or other stress reduction activity because you were busy. Maybe you had a job interview but didn't get the job. Maybe you skipped your forms, or your exercises, or you didn't carry out your action plan for the day. Things happen.

Change is rarely smooth, easy, and perfect. And that is okay. What is important is how you think about setbacks and handle them.

Apply the thinking skills you learned for using with panic. Treat a setback as an AFOG (Another Fabulous Opportunity for Growth). How can you think about a setback in a way that is both true and helpful? What helpful lesson you can learn from it. Review Chapter 12: Learn Sensations Are Safe for details.

You Have a Right to Get Better

I realize that at times I am asking you to do things that scare you. Remind yourself that thousands of people have used this approach to overcome anxiety and panic. This approach is used successfully all over the world and I have personally seen this program help many, many people. Think about *what you have to gain*.

You *want to get better* or you would not have read this far. I believe *you deserve to get better*. No one should live in the shadow of fear, frightened of anxiety or panic. I encourage you to start taking steps and begin the process of change.

Happily Ever After

"I feel like I am cured. It's amazing. It's fabulous." – Jasmine

"I am so much happier." — Taylor

In this section, you will have the opportunity to pause and reflect on what you have learned and where you are now compared to when you started this program. You will catch up with Amanda, Raj, Liah, and Carlos. And you will find tips on maintaining your positive changes.

Chapter **15:**

Living Free of Anxiety and Panic

"I'm glad I came to this therapy. It was life-changing." — *Chris*

"Life is good now." – *Juan*

"I feel like myself again! I don't feel trapped by the whole idea of panic any more. I have the tools if and when it happens." – *Sarah*

"I'm excited to go out and do things now and I hadn't felt that way for years. It had just been dread and thinking, 'Do I have to leave the house?'" – *Maria*

I hope you have been deliberately facing your fears. What changes do you notice as you review your Form 8-02: Anxiety Records (page 110) and Form 8-03: Panic Records (page 114)? What patterns do you see?

What You Have Learned

You have learned your personal triggers for anxiety or panic. You understand what happens in your brain when these triggers are hit, and how and why your brain creates anxiety or panic sensations in your body. You have learned how fear and danger thoughts and fear-based actions create and maintain a vicious cycle.

You have also learned how to *break* your anxiety/panic cycle. I have guided you through a series of steps to overcome anxiety and panic:

1. Learning about panic and the anxiety cycle and gaining a deep understanding of your personal anxiety cycle. Your experience should begin to make sense now that you understand how panic and anxiety work.

2. Reducing your anxiety triggers.

3. Responding differently to anxiety or panic sensations when they are triggered using tools like accept, belly breathe, and chart.

4. Changing your thinking by identifying, articulating, and analyzing your panic thoughts, using your Thinking Brain to evaluate and question your fears, getting the relevant facts, comparing fear to facts, and replacing panic thoughts with thoughts that are both true and helpful. Making and following coping plans for true alarms.

5. Discovering that anxiety or panic sensations are harmless through deliberate, scheduled, repeated practice of the physical exercises and noticing what happens and what you learn.

6. *Acting on the facts*, not the fears, by facing activities or situations that scare your Reacting Brain and repeatedly showing it that you are safe and can cope. Having courage, taking risks, and turning every episode of panic, fear, or anxiety into an AFOG (Another F**** Opportunity for Growth)!

Review Your Progress

Your goal was to overcome panic, break your anxiety cycle, and live your life freely without fearing panic. How are you doing? Review and evaluate your progress by filling out Form 15-01: Progress Review (page 267) and Form 15-02: Anxiety or Panic Sensations (page 271).

If you have achieved your goal already, congratulations! Continue doing what is working for you and read the section "Maintain Your Progress" below.

If you have made progress, congratulations! Continue following the program. Track your progress. Work on the areas you want to improve.

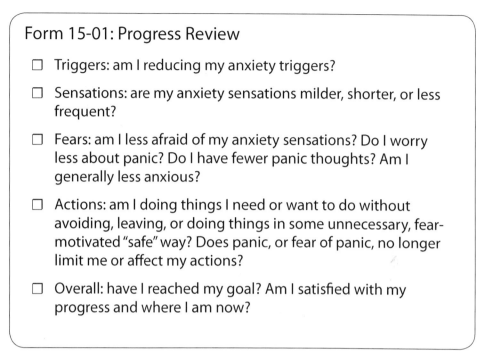

Form 15-01: Progress Review

- ☐ Triggers: am I reducing my anxiety triggers?

- ☐ Sensations: are my anxiety sensations milder, shorter, or less frequent?

- ☐ Fears: am I less afraid of my anxiety sensations? Do I worry less about panic? Do I have fewer panic thoughts? Am I generally less anxious?

- ☐ Actions: am I doing things I need or want to do without avoiding, leaving, or doing things in some unnecessary, fear-motivated "safe" way? Does panic, or fear of panic, no longer limit me or affect my actions?

- ☐ Overall: have I reached my goal? Am I satisfied with my progress and where I am now?

Story: Amanda

Amanda continues to be panic-free and happily shops at the mall on a regular basis. She has a much better understanding of her anxiety cycle and actively works to keep her anxiety triggers in check. She is more assertive with her mother, while accepting that in some ways her mother will never change. Amanda deliberately focuses on what she is grateful for. She accepts that there is uncertainty in life and that she will occasionally feel worried about something. However, now she makes a plan to cope with those situations which helps her get through those times with less panic, worry, or distress.

Story: Raj

Raj is doing well and enjoying his job much more now that he is no longer afraid to eat with co-workers. He realized all the fun he was missing by not joining his colleagues for meals. He is able to manage his commute with his revised work schedule and is much more relaxed and calmer with his fam-

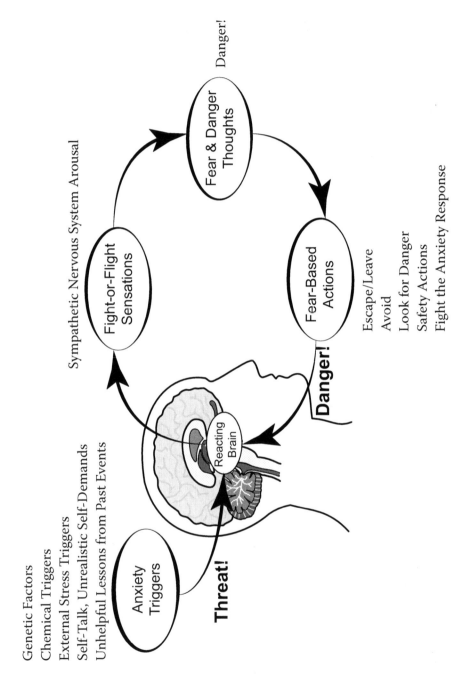

Figure 15-01: Anxiety Cycle

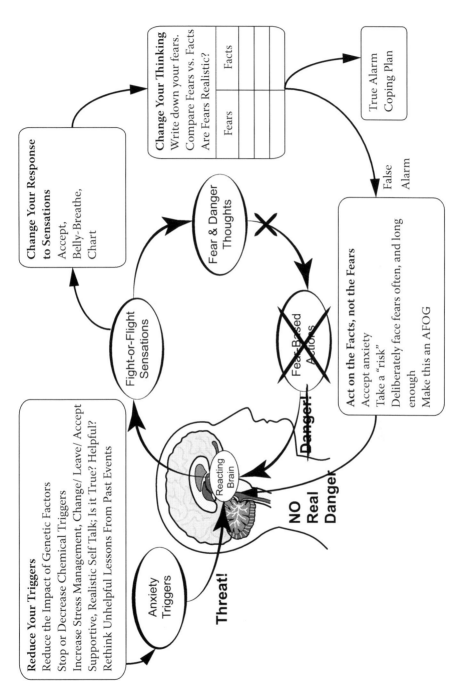

Figure 15-02: Breaking the Anxiety Cycle

Form 15-02: Anxiety or Panic Sensations (next page)

During the past week, how much were you bothered by these sensations while feeling anxious or panicky? Rate each sensation using this 0-3 scale:

0 None, did not happen or did not bother me

1 Mild, bothered me a little but not much

2 Moderate, bothered me and was unpleasant at times

3 Severe, this sensation bothered me a lot

---

ily. Raj told us that his son remarked, "Dad, I'm glad you got help for your anxiety because you are a lot more fun now!"

Story: Liah

Liah is also living a more balanced life. She drinks less coffee, no longer takes work home, and spends more time relaxing and exercising on the weekends. She continues to challenge her "perfectionistic self-demands" by reminding herself that she is doing the best she can. She made great progress in facing her feared sensations and no longer panics during her drive to work on Monday mornings. In fact, she recently sent us a note that said "Thank you! Thank you! I feel lighter and freer. Life is so much better!"

Story: Carlos

Carlos practiced his physical exercises with dedication and was happy to tell us that his anxiety levels had dropped quickly. He very rarely has panic thoughts when his heart starts racing or he starts feeling hot and sweaty. He realizes now that the physical sensations are harmless and that he is not having a heart attack. There are occasional times when his Reacting Brain gets activated and tries to convince him that something is medically wrong. However, Carlos is able to use the skills he's learned to challenge these panic thoughts with facts and logic and his anxiety quickly decreases. Now Carlos

Form 15-02: Anxiety or Panic Sensations

Sensation	Rating 0-3
Fast heartbeat, racing or pounding heart	
Chest tightness or chest pain	
Muscle tension	
Scared, nervous, afraid	
Fear of dying	
Fear of worst happening	
Feeling shaky, trembling, or weak	
Feeling unsteady	
Fear of losing control	
Short of breath, like you can't breathe, or not getting enough air	
Feeling hot or flushed	
Sweaty or clammy	
Tingling, numbness, or feeling cold	
Dizzy, unsteady, light-headed, or faint	
Visual changes like blurriness, spots, dark, light, tunnel vision, etc.	
Feeling unreal or like you are not present	
Nausea, queasiness, butterflies, knots in your stomach, other abdominal symptoms	
Feeling of choking, lump in the throat, can't swallow	
Feeling like you cannot think or concentrate	

Other physical sensations:

_____

_____

is enjoying his retirement and spending many wonderful moments with his family.

Maintain Your Progress

If you are satisfied with your progress, you want things to stay that way. Keep doing what you are doing. Do not fall back into avoiding, escaping, or taking safety actions. Keep your Thinking Brain strong and in charge. Be patient, but very firm, with the Reacting Brain.

Keep practicing belly breathing. Use it often, especially if you are tense.

Take care of yourself. Get enough sleep. Eat the right amounts of a variety of healthy foods and drinks. Exercise and be active. Use good stress management. Support your physical and mental health. Keep positive activities and supportive people in your life.

Once a month, fill out a Form 8-02: Anxiety Record (page 110) or redo Form 15-01: Progress Review (page 267). Review and work on specific topics, as needed.

Reread parts of this book as often as you need. The tools and the information are here for you.

If your triggers increase or you stop facing activities, anxiety can return. You probably already know what I am going to say, "Treat this as an AFOG."

If Anxiety Symptoms Return

Remind yourself that panic is a *natural response* when your triggers are hit, or if something re-activates your anxiety cycle. Reassure yourself that anxiety is a fact of life and that panic is not dangerous.

Go back over the anxiety cycle and think about your current situation. Look for any anxiety triggers, fear thoughts, and/or fear-based actions. Explore what is happening or what has changed, and problem solve using the skills you have learned.

Review Your Personal Anxiety Triggers

Changes in triggers can sometimes revive anxiety. Review the triggers you identified in Chapter 3 Your Anxiety Triggers and look for changes:

- Do you have any chemical triggers? Have you changed what you eat, drink, or smoke? Have you changed the drugs or supplements you take? If you are female, have your hormone levels changed?

- Has there been an increase in external stress? Have other stresses crept into your life? Often stress builds up gradually and unnoticed until it reaches a level that triggers anxiety or panic. What has changed in your life? Have there been changes in job, family life, relationships, finances, living situation? Are people making unrealistic demands of you or being negative or critical toward you?

- Write down every possible source of stress—even stresses you have been dealing with for a while. Remember the "boiled frog syndrome" (see page 66).

- Has your self-talk gotten negative or critical? Have your self-demands become unrealistic? Are you depressed (see page 8 for the Depression Checklist)?

- Is your Reacting Brain reacting to an unhelpful lesson from the past? Has something happened to you—or to someone you know—that may be triggering anxiety? Did you recently read about or hear about something bad or frightening happening that could have set off your Reacting Brain? Was there a recent anniversary of a death, illness, loss, or other stressful past event? Did something happen to re-activate unhelpful lessons from your past?

Look for Something You Haven't Done Recently

Symptoms may return if you have not faced a certain activity or situation for a while. You may feel less confident and have a little anxiety when you face it again. This is nothing to worry about.

People often report feeling more anxious if it has been some time since they did a particular activity or were in a particular situation. Even if you were not avoiding out of fear, you may notice some panic if it has been a while since you last drove on a highway or in a crowded city, flew on a plane, talked to a group, attended a party, gave a report or presentation, performed, etc.

Anything you have not done recently may temporarily make your Reacting Brain more worried and alert to possible dangers or problems. Use the skills you have learned. Use your Thinking Brain to calm, override, and reprogram your Reacting Brain.

Story: Amanda

Amanda needed some minor foot surgery so she could not work or drive for several weeks. The surgery and recovery went well, and she was fine, "I did not even worry about having a panic attack or something going wrong in surgery."

It was stressful being home with her mother and the children and worrying about finances. Because she was looking forward to getting back to work, she was really surprised when she had panic symptoms driving to work for her first day back.

The old fears about driving had temporarily returned, but now she knew what to do. She reviewed this book, practiced belly breathing, reminded herself of the facts, and kept driving. The more she drove, the more confident and relaxed she became.

Look for Something New

Symptoms may return when you start a new activity or situation. For example, panic attacks may be triggered by starting a new school, a new grade, a new job, a new relationship, or any different activity. You may notice anxiety after a promotion, a retirement, a move, etc. This is annoying, but understandable.

As the activity or situation becomes more familiar, your confidence will increase, and your nervousness will fade away. To speed that process, use the skills you have learned.

Repeat What Helped Before

When panic or anxiety symptoms return for any reason, reread this book, especially the parts that helped before, or parts that apply to your current situation.

What worked before should work again. In fact, it will probably work even more quickly, because you have more knowledge and skill than you had when you started.

You have already had some success in dealing with panic. No matter how strongly your panic may flare up, you will never be back where you started because of everything you have done and learned since then.

Review your past records. What sensations or activities used to frighten you? How did you get over your fear? Remember what you did that helped you in the past. Use the same approach to cope with current anxiety.

If you have a new sensation, reread Chapter 5: Your Anxiety or Panic Sensations and Chapter 10: Change Your Response to Sensations.

If you have a new fear (or an old fear has returned), reread Chapter 6: Your Fear and Danger Thoughts and Chapter 11: Change Your Thinking and use the skills. Identify your fears. Get the facts. Review the facts. Practice changing from fear-based panic thinking to fact-based true and helpful thinking.

If you are avoiding, leaving, or doing something only in a "safe way," reread Chapter 13: Learn Activities Are Safe and use those skills. If an activity makes you anxious because you haven't done it in a while, begin to deliberately practice it as often as possible. Act on the facts, not the fear.

If a therapist or group therapy helped you before, consider going back for a refresher. If you think something physically wrong is causing anxiety or panic, check with your healthcare provider.

Take Good Care

Congratulations for caring about your mental health and well-being. Take full credit for your progress and success.

If you want to share your experience and your comments, I would be very interested in hearing from you. Please send comments to Elizabeth@Elizabeth-McMahon.com.

I would also love to hear what you liked about the book and what was helpful. Share your success story, it will make my day.

I am equally interested in hearing suggestions on what would make this book better. What was not helpful? What changes would you like to see? What parts did you dislike?

Please let others know if you recommend this book by posting online reviews or sharing on social media.

I wish you all the best. May you and your caveman Reacting Brain live together happily in today's modern world!

Take care,

Elizabeth McMahon

Appendix

Finding a Therapist

I recommend that you look for a licensed mental health professional with specific training in cognitive behavioral therapy (CBT) for anxiety and panic. Ideally you want a therapist whose treatment approach and recommendations are consistent with what you have learned here. CBT for anxiety and panic may be provided as individual or group therapy.

Ideally a therapist should:

- Be a licensed mental health professional or supervised by a licensed professional.

- Have experience using CBT specifically for anxiety and panic issues.

- Make you feel comfortable, understood, cared about, and respected.

- Explain things in ways you understand and that make sense to you.

- Be encouraging.

- Treat you as an active partner in your therapy.

- Monitor your progress.

- Problem-solve with you if you are not making progress.

Types of Therapists

Licensing requirements for mental health professionals vary from state to state. Being *licensed* means a therapist meets the state's legal requirements for training and may have had to pass examinations. Be aware that labels like "psychotherapist", "therapist", and "counselor" are *not* legally defined terms. People using these titles without listing a professional designation or license *may not be* qualified or licensed.

There are many types of licensed mental health professionals including:

- Psychologists who are trained and qualified to provide comprehensive mental health services and have a PhD or PsyD degree.

- Psychiatrists who are medical doctors (MD) with additional training in psychotherapy and psychopharmacology. Many psychiatrists primarily provide medication-based treatments.

- Mental health professionals with training in therapy and/or counseling. In California these include Licensed Marriage and Family Therapists (LMFT), Licensed Clinical Social Workers (LCSW), Licensed Educational Psychologists (LEP) and Licensed Professional Clinical Counselors (LPCC).

Looking 'In-Network'

Most health insurance providers or health maintenance organizations provide mental health benefits that can be used to pay for this type of therapy. To find a therapist who may be covered by your insurance, ask your health insurance provider for the names of licensed mental health providers who are part of their network.

If you are covered by a Health Savings Account (HSA), you may be able to use this account to pay for psychotherapy. Ask your HSA administrator if this benefit is restricted to in-network providers.

Searching Online

To search online for a therapist, you can look for specific search results, check the major therapist locator websites, and search local therapist locator websites for therapists near you, as explained below.

Search online using a search engine such as Google.com, Bing.com, Yahoo.com, or the local equivalents if you are outside the US. Use combinations of search terms indicating the type of service and/or type of therapist, and the geographic location where you live or areas where you would be willing to go for treatment.

Therapist availability varies greatly in different areas. You can adjust for this by starting with very specific search terms and then changing to more general terms if you do not find many search results.

Examples of search terms from specific to more general:

- Service: anxiety treatment, panic treatment, cognitive behavioral therapy, psychotherapy, mental health services, etc.

- Therapist type: clinical psychologist, psychologist, clinical social worker, etc. Check the types of therapists licensed in your state as discussed above and add these to your search.

- Location as Zip Code (in the US) or postal code, neighborhood, town or city, metropolitan area, county or region, state or province, etc. Some search engines support location shortcuts like 'near me' but you may need to correct your location on the search results page.

Modify the service terms if you are looking for treatment for other conditions such as depression, post-traumatic stress disorder, etc. If you want treatment for a specific fear or phobia include that topic. For example: treatment for fear of flying, fear of heights, public speaking anxiety, needle phobia, etc.

If you are looking for a therapist who offers virtual reality therapy (see page 250), include "virtual reality therapy" or "virtual reality exposure therapy" in your search criteria. When screening therapists, describe the issues for which you would like to use virtual reality, and ask whether the therapist has access to the appropriate virtual environments. For example: virtual reality treatment for fear of flying or virtual reality therapy for fear of flying.

Major Therapist Locator Websites

Major therapist locator websites in North America include:

- American Psychological Association www.apa.org

- Anxiety and Depression Association of America: www.adaa.org

- Association for Behavioral and Cognitive Therapies: www.abct.org

- Canadian Mental Health Association: www.cmha.ca.

- Psychology Today: www.psychologytoday.com

- United States government directory of local mental health treatment services: www.mentalhealth.gov

Typically, these sites allow searching by type of service and geographical location.

Local Therapist Locators

Local therapist locator websites would include state or local professional organizations for licensed mental health professionals. These vary widely and these organization may not exist in all areas or offer this type of directory.

For example, to find a psychologist in San Francisco, California, you might look at these websites:

- California Psychological Association (www.cpapsych.org), and the

- San Francisco Psychological Association (www.sfpa.net).

To find local websites in your area, search for "psychological association" together with the name of your town, region, state or province.

Share Your Work

When you go to meet with your therapist, take this book and all your forms and records with you. Any work that you have done on your own can help your therapy go more quickly.

Index

A

Adrenaline 21, 29, 30, 68, 75, 76, 82, 87, 88, 100, 147
AFOG 195, 255, 262, 266, 272
Agoraphobia 32
Alcohol 44, 126, 130
Alcoholics Anonymous 127
Alcoholism 43, 44
Alprazolam 35, 46, 248, 249
Amanda 9, 12, 14, 18, 43, 50, 58, 92, 103, 105, 125, 141, 175, 187, 267, 274
Ambien 33
American Psychological Association 280
Amygdala 21, 33
Anabolic steroids 46
Android 150, 257
Anti-anxiety medications 35, 46, 212, 248, 253
Anti-depressants 46
Antony, Martin 287
Anxiety 3, 7, 19, 32, 64, 277
Anxiety and Depression Association of America 280
Anxiety attacks 6, 9, 12, 19, 32, 77, 83, 100
Anxiety cycle 19, 35, 39, 41, 60, 95, 108, 115, 121, 145, 153
Anxiety model 1, 107

Anxiety or panic sensations 6, 21, 64, 71, 108, 121, 166, 197, 258
Anxiety Records 13, 108, 111, 115, 126, 145, 154, 157, 189, 229, 244, 265
Anxiety triggers 5, 19, 30, 35, 41, 60, 63, 95, 121, 123, 266, 272
Apps
belly breathing 150
Breathe2Relax 150, 257
relaxation 150
Association for Behavioral and Cognitive Therapies 280
Asthma 36, 203
Asthma inhalers 46
Ativan 35, 248, 249
Attention deficit disorder meds 46
Atwood, Margaret 128
Avoiding or leaving 32, 101, 104, 237, 254, 258, 267, 272, 275

B

Barlow, David 287
Beck, Aaron 287
Belly breathing 64, 78, 130, 147, 150, 153, 256, 272
Belsomra 33
Benzodiazepines 35, 46
Betablockers 46
Bing.com 279

L
Lantz, DeLee 287
Lerner, Uma 287
Liah 11, 13, 14, 43, 47, 48, 53, 58,
    65, 104, 105, 125, 136, 142,
    163, 176, 177, 222, 270
Loneliness 48
Lorazepam 35, 248, 249
Lunesta 33
Lung disease 203

M
Marijuana 44, 45, 126
Medical conditions 36
Medications 34, 36, 44, 126
Meditation 130, 149
Meichenbaum, Donald 287
Menstrual cycle 47
Mental health professional 7, 17,
    57, 138, 140, 150, 252, 255,
    277
Methamphetamines 46
Mindfulness 130
Mitral valve prolapse 36
Muscle relaxation 130, 147
Muscle tension 74

N
Negative self-talk 51, 61, 66, 173
Nicotine 44, 45, 130
Non-prescription drugs 46

O
Obsessive-compulsive behaviors 32
Obsessive-compulsive disorder 36,
    255
Overbreathing 64, 76, 148
Overcoming anxiety 3, 6
Oxygen/carbon dioxide balance 64,
    76, 147

P
Padesky, Christine 287
Palpitations 44, 74
Panic 19, 277
  during sleep 64

unexpected 63
while relaxing 63
Panic actions 98, 153
Panic aftereffects 84
Panic attacks 3, 6, 19, 26, 29, 30,
    32, 36, 41, 54, 60, 146, 253,
    255
Panic disorder 32, 36
Panic fears 88, 168
Panic Records 13, 84, 109, 111,
    115, 145, 153, 157, 160, 163,
    171, 189, 229, 232, 244, 255,
    265
Panic response 34, 62, 66, 80, 157,
    193
Paper forms 6
Parasympathetic nervous system
    147
Past events 19, 54, 56, 61, 101, 138,
    173
Past event triggers 54, 136
Perfectionism 53
Physical exercises 197, 258, 266
Physical sensations 29, 35, 44, 64,
    88, 163, 166, 197
Positive psychology 3
Post-traumatic stress 32
Post-traumatic stress disorder 36,
    57, 138, 251, 252, 255
Prescription medications 46
Psychology Today 280

Q
Qi gong 130

R
Raj 10, 13, 14, 48, 56, 103, 105,
    131, 141, 210, 216, 220, 267
Reacting Brain 19, 21, 23, 24, 25,
    26, 28, 29, 30, 33, 35, 54, 61,
    63, 64, 65, 68, 74, 76, 77, 78,
    79, 80, 81, 84, 87, 88, 92, 98,
    100, 101, 111, 115, 132, 136,
    138, 139, 140, 145, 147, 151,
    153, 157, 159, 160, 165, 166,

Acknowledgements

I would like to acknowledge the many clinicians, researchers, and teachers in the field of psychotherapy from whom I have learned and whose research and writings have informed my practice and form the foundation of this book including (in alphabetical order) Martin Antony, PhD, David Barlow, PhD, Aaron Beck, MD, David Burns, MD, Michelle Craske, PhD, Albert Ellis, PhD, Donald Meichenbaum, PhD, and Christine Padesky, PhD.

Thanks are due to all the reviewers who took time from very busy schedules to comment on this material; especially Gary Dykstra, MD and Uma Lerner, MD for reviewing the medication information; DeLee Lantz, PhD and Chris Gilbert, PhD for reviewing the information on overbreathing; and Shawn Giammattei, PhD, Lara Honos-Webb, PhD, Robin Rosenberg, PhD, ABPP and Charlotte Tilson, PsyD for sharing their expertise and reviewing portions of the manuscript. Their suggestions improved the accuracy, any remaining errors are my own.

Similarly, thanks are due to the wonderful colleagues and post-doctoral psychology residents I had the very great pleasure of working with at the Kaiser Permanente Medical Center in Fremont, California. Thank you to all of you who served as co-leaders in the anxiety and panic therapy groups.

Special thanks to Lindsey Kremmel, PhD for help with the case examples. Your involvement and support helped bring this book to fruition and your feedback on the earlier drafts made it better.

Heartfelt thanks go to all my clients who used earlier drafts of this workbook and provided feedback and suggestions. Your positive comments gave me a reason to persevere. Your courage and resilience are inspiring.

Finally, a big acknowledgement to my husband for his emotional and practical support throughout the process of writing. This book would not be possible without you.

About the Author

Elizabeth McMahon, PhD

Dr. McMahon is a clinical psychologist who specializes in helping people overcome anxiety-related issues. Currently she sees a limited number of clients in private practice, teaches, writes, and lectures.

She has been using virtual reality (VR) technology with clients since 2010 and is working with the National Mental Health Innovation Center to improve treatment options for anxiety. She trains therapists on anxiety treatment and the use of VR in continuing education courses organized by APA, CPA, PESI, and VR technology providers.

Dr. McMahon has been practicing for over 40 years including working for Kaiser Permanente Medical Group in Fremont California, a post-doctoral residency at Sheppard-Pratt Psychiatric Hospital in Baltimore Maryland, and a pre-doctoral fellowship at the University of Virginia Medical Center in Charlottesville Virginia.

She received her MA and PhD degrees in psychology from Case Western Reserve University and her BA in Psychology from Earlham College.

Her website is www.elizabeth-mcmahon.com.

Made in the USA
Columbia, SC
23 May 2020